CHOOSE LIFE!

Awareness and practical empowerment workbook for survivors of childhood sexual abuse

Yvonne Ellis

CHOOSE LIFE!

Scripture Quotations noted NKJV and NIV are taken from the New King James version and New International Version of the bible

Copyright© Yvonne Ellis/YEME Empowerment

London/England
www.yemeempowerment.com

Book Layout ©2018 Bookhelpline.co.uk

Yvonne Ellis/Choose life. —
ISBN 978-1-9998590-1-5

ACKNOWLEDGEMENTS

I would like to thank first and foremost the architect of my healing and journey to recovery, Jesus Christ. Through my Heavenly Father I have been able to overcome many challenges and experienced many victories thus far. I am truly grateful for the opportunities I had to heal, learn, support and help others.

I would like to thank my husband, Stephen Ellis, for his support; my daughter Jada for her warm hugs; and Niki Fayese, Ije Stoddart, Andrena Palmer, Pauline Brown, and Llewelyn and Carol Richards for their continued encouragement, prayers and support.

CONTENTS

FOREWORD

Sexual abuse is a term most people don't like to say out loud. It's a term that is whispered under our breath when we think no one will hear us. It speaks volumes and causes so much pain. It tears families apart, bruises the soul, causes fear and anger and overwhelming guilt, and renders us powerless. The psychological wounds left by sexual abuse can take decades to heal and the stigma it carries can make the strongest of us feel quite uncomfortable. It's for this very reason that it has been kept hidden for so long, and only recently, due to the deafening outcry, that the world has been forced to stop and listen, and incidents of sexual abuse have finally been taken seriously. The outcome is people who have experienced sexual abuse are now finding a voice and speaking out about the damage and pain they suffered at the hands of their abusers, which is helping more and more people – young and old, male and female – to speak out about their own experiences and the injustice and horror of sexual abuse

'Choose Life' by Yvonne Ellis is a truly remarkable book that not only gives personal, factual and educational insight into sexual abuse, but also the tools to empower the reader and survivors of sexual abuse to get the help and support needed to move forward. Throughout her book, Yvonne stands on strong biblical principles and the Word of God. Yvonne speaks about the power of 'choice' being in our hands, learning to forgive, and walks us through the process of healing through the love of Jesus Christ. Yvonne not only writes graphically about her own experience of being sexually abused as a child but walks us through her personal and intimate journey of healing, empowering the reader to take back control of their life through professional and practical steps.

As an experienced Integrative CBT Psychodynamic,

Person Centred Counsellor, and registered member of the BACP, who has been in private practice for over ten years, I whole heartedly endorse this book as a great self-help tool for people who have experienced sexual abuse whether as a child or as an adult and who want greater insight into sexual abuse and the tools to start the process of healing. As someone who has worked closely with Yvonne over many years, I know that she has poured her heart and soul into this book; she is passionate about helping people who have been sexually abused to find their voice, and helping to educate and equip them to take back control and Choose Life.

Sheree Pinheiro MBACP

INTRODUCTION

As a survivor of childhood sexual abuse, I have learned so much about myself since I first spoke out twenty-eight years ago. For many years my experience led me to believe that I was worth nothing more than what my abuse left me feeling: worthless, weak, unlovable and used. I did not realise my view of self was tainted because of the trauma I had experienced as a child, and that because I operated out of a mindset of hopelessness, it allowed an open door for other people at times to use and abuse me. My mind became a breeding ground that allowed a repetitive cycle of destructive emotions to culminate in behaviour that only served to validate the negative feelings held deep inside me.

It is only through a relationship with Jesus Christ that I have found the courage to step out from behind the mask of fear, rejection and shame that kept me captive for so long. I no longer see myself as a hopeless case. When I look in the mirror, I see a courageous, strong, valuable, creative and lovable woman who, in spite of much adversity, has overcome many challenges. I see a woman not only has a lot to offer those closest to her and her immediate community but also, I believe, the world.

The journey to healing from abuse at times has been painful and hard, but also empowering. As I have faced each revelation and challenge head-on, gaining victory over what has hindered me, The Living God has helped me experience real breakthrough in helping me find my identity. Each memory, fear, and feeling of pain held within me has slowly been released and healed through my faith in Jesus – he is my cornerstone and strength in enabling me to be resilient and determined to claim back my life.

I liken the process of healing from childhood sexual abuse to the analogy of an onion: as I have walked through the steps to restoration, each peeled back layer has revealed fears, insecurities, hidden memories and psychological effects that stood in the way of me getting to know who I really was. Each layer of past experience is interjected with the blurred memory of the promise of the young woman I could have grown up to be before that promise was thwarted. Forgotten and buried deep within the trauma that sought to eclipse my soul, I had to make a choice to fight not only for my survival but also against the misconceptions society has about what a survivor of sexual abuse is supposed to be in the aftermath. It is by the grace of God, with courage and time on my side, that I have got to where I am today. By facing each challenge one at a time, things that I thought were impossible to get over, I have overcome. With God, all things are possible.

No matter where you are on your journey to restoration and healing, my hope is this book can support you at whatever stage you find yourself. I am not a counsellor or therapist – I am just someone who wants to share and use my experiences to support and help others who have been through similar experiences to me. The aim of this self-help workbook, which has been written by me from a survivor's perspective, is to provide you with information concerning issues surrounding sexual abuse and its aftermath, and to give commentary and insight from my point of view to raise awareness and to help you on your journey to healing.

My intention in presenting both factual and personal information is to empower you to believe you can overcome your past. This is not fantasy or a trip into wishful thinking – I am living proof that it is possible. I am truthful about how my experiences affected me at different stages of my life, and I have included diary entries and poems from a certain period of my life to show you a small glimpse of the battles I was going through. I have included self-help exercises, affirmations and declarations created by me from things I found helpful over the years, and pose questions to get you thinking about your experience and journey. I have written this book to encourage you. Whilst engaging in the writing exercises, be honest and be open, for the aim is to empower you. You don't have to share what you write – unless you want to. It is completely up to you; it is your choice.

I believe the trauma of childhood sexual abuse tends to have a detrimental impact on thought and decision processes, and therefore potentially becomes an obstacle in moving beyond the past. I have found this to be true from my own experience and the years I have spent supporting other survivors. It proves very difficult to make positive and productive decisions when you are emotionally

4

wounded and feeling hopeless. What is needed in these times of emotional instability and uncertainty is a foundation of truth to stand on; something outside of self that you can stand firm on in times of personal crisis. The biggest step and decision you will need to make first is to acknowledge what has happened to you, for it is in doing this that the future you desire will become attainable. It is a gradual process of transformation and change, but in acknowledging and taking the steps to free yourself from the prison of your past you will make space in your heart and mind to envision your future hopes and dreams; you can and will have a promising future.

For I know the plans I have towards you, plans to give you hope and a good future – Jeremiah 29:11

Yvonne

TERMINOLOGIES USED

Terminologies that I use in this book in relation to sexual abuse:

First of all, I do need to warn you that because of the nature of the topic you may find it stirs up emotional or physical responses and/or flashbacks of memories. This is often described as being 'triggered'. Even though I do not go into explicit details of my experience, because I am trying to raise awareness and bring insight into the issue of sexual abuse, I do talk about it in an open and frank manner to highlight its seriousness. My intention is not to shock or alarm you but to expose the stark reality of what childhood sexual abuse really entails.

Empower point: Self-help action point exercises throughout the book for you to engage in.

Victim: Commonly used in reference to individuals who have been a victim of crime – in this instance, sexual abuse.

Survivor: Commonly used to describe victims of non-fatal harm – in this instance, sexual abuse. To survive means you have lived through your abuse, and the term intends to honour and empower the strength of the individual to heal.

Perpetrator and **Abuser:** Both words refer to someone who commits the act of sexual abuse.

Thriver: A word used to describe an individual who has not only survived their experience, but has gone on to succeed and excel in their life goals.

However you see yourself – victim, survivor or thriver – it is personal to you. We have all been the victims of childhood sexual abuse but depending on where you are in your healing will affect how you view yourself; hopefully that will change over time.

ENCOURAGEMENT FROM A FRIEND

You know me, and you know that what I say to you will never be empty words or intended to harm you. This is just a card to bring you some encouragement.

Every change starts in your mind and your attitude, for your thoughts will dictate which way you go IN SPITE of the things that's has happened in your life.

Reclaim what's yours…Your LIFE.

(Card sent to me by a friend nineteen years ago)

CHILD

(Poem I wrote in January 2000)

I feel alone,

I need someone in my life

No, I thought I needed my Mum

No, I thought I needed my Dad

But how can I want these things

When it's something I never had

Yvonne

PART ONE – SEXUAL ABUSE

THE THING CALLED 'IT'

That was the only way I could describe what happened to me at such a young age. I was 9 years old when 'it' intruded on my life and it never left. The little girl I was before it came – full of playful fun – was suddenly gone. It was my fault – that is what I believed for the longest time. If only I had not lied and said I was sick so I could stay home from school, this would not have happened. I had it all worked out in my little head. Mum would stay home and look after me and we could spend time together, but instead Dad offered to stay home while she went to work.

I was watching TV downstairs when I heard him call me from their bedroom upstairs. I assumed he was calling me to give me chores such as washing dishes, but nothing could have prepared me for what he did. As I entered into my parents' bedroom, my dad, who was lying in the bed he shared with my mum, told me to get into bed with him. He was naked. It was then he raped me.

Something died within me at that moment when he violated me. My life was never the same again after the day my dad, a man who was supposed to love and protect me, crossed the line and did the unthinkable.

To this day I cannot articulate or describe the change that happened to me. I sensed danger on entering the room, but because of the unfamiliarity of the situation and because I was a child, I just obeyed. I was under attack but did not know what I was being attacked with; I only knew that the person who was committing the attack on me was someone I loved. It was not a one-off incident and the attacks continued frequently, with my dad invading my space every opportunity he got. He even carried out these attacks in eye view of Mum by coming into the bathroom as I had my evening wash. There was no way she could not have seen him entering or leaving the bathroom – it was opposite their bedroom. Most evenings she sat on the bed with the bedroom door open whilst she watched TV. I came to the realisation many years later that she knew what he was doing.

From the age of 9 to 13 years old my dad violated and raped me numerous times. Being sexually abused brought so much turmoil into my life, and the suddenness of these assaults left me in a constant state of being alert, feeling anxious and scared. I found it hard to concentrate and keep focused on my work at school. Fear manifested itself in constant stomach aches and I believed I was dying because of the overwhelming trauma I was suffering. My behaviour deteriorated as I lied, cheated and stole from my parents and from shops. My emotions and behaviour were unpredictable, going from one extreme to the next like a pendulum swinging from manic false happiness to suicidal depressive lows. I became emotionally numb and despondent during the five years I suffered sexual abuse. I learned to disassociate myself from the rapes by letting my mind take me to another place far from where I was, which was suffocating and in pain under the weight of my dad. The thing called 'IT' overwhelmed and controlled every aspect of my life until that unforgettable day when Childline came to my secondary school. Finally, its ugliness was revealed: sexual abuse.

WHAT IS SEXUAL ABUSE?

Sexual abuse is described by the NSPCC (National Society of Prevention of Cruelty to Children) as when 'a child is forced or persuaded to take part in sexual activities'. It is not a new phenomenon and is present in every country worldwide. It occurs in all racial, ethnic, religious and socioeconomic groups and affects children of all ages, including infants. Sexual abuse falls into two categories: contact and non-contact.

Contact abuse involves touching activities where the abuser makes physical contact with the child, including penetration. This includes:
- Sexual touching of any part of the child's body whether clothed or not;
- Rape or penetration by putting an object or body part inside a child's vagina, mouth or anus;
- Forcing or encouraging a child to take part in sexual activity;
- Making a child take their clothes off, touch someone else's genitals or masturbate.

Non-contact abuse involves non-touching activities, such as grooming, exploitation, persuading children to perform sexual acts and flashing. This includes:

- Encouraging a child to watch or hear sexual acts;
- Not taking proper measures to prevent a child being exposed to sexual activities of others;
- Meeting a child following sexual grooming with the intent to abuse them;
- Online abuse including making, viewing or distributing child abuse images;
- Allowing someone else to make, view or distribute child abuse images;
- Showing pornography to a child;
- Sexually exploiting a child for money, power or status; sexual coercion.

The statistics are alarming for child sexual abuse:

- 1 in 20 children have been sexually abused; (Figures based on findings on 11–17-year-olds; source, Radford, L. et al. 2011);
- 1 in 25 boys are sexually abused; (Statistics courtesy of www.darknesstolight.org, USA)
- 1 in 7 girls are sexually abused. (Statistics courtesy of www.darknesstolight.org, USA)

Other forms of sexual abuse that can take place face-to-face or online are:

Child Sexual Exploitation. This involves a child being in an exploitative situation or relationship (*older male, female, someone physically stronger*) where they receive gifts, money or affection as a result of performing sexual acts or others performing sexual acts on them. Common age group is 13–15 years old but children 10–13 years old have been affected. (*Intro to CSE – Barnardo's*)

Grooming. This is when someone builds up an emotional connection with the child to gain trust for the purpose of sexual abuse, trafficking and exploitation.

It is important to note that 90% of sexual abuse is committed by someone the child knows, loves or trusts.

According to the *Office of National Crime Statistics report*, year ending 2016, the top 9 groups by which sexual assault and penetration attempts were carried out on a child aged 16 and under where:

27% Friend or acquaintance

23% Other family members

16% Stranger

15% Person of trust or authority (teacher, doctor, youth worker, carer)

11% Someone else

8% Stepfather

5% Father

2% Mother

1% Partner or previous partner

It important to note not only men sexually abuse children; women do too. The percentage (2%), although small, is just as serious a problem but not as commonly highlighted as in male perpetrator cases. It is hard to fathom that a woman, who by nature is perceived as a nurturer and care giver, could sexually abuse a child; but as we have seen in media news reports, female teachers, child minders, mothers and nursery workers have been convicted of and jailed for child sexual abuse.

Graham Wilmer, founder of the Lantern Project, who was once appointed an adviser to the independent government panel on sexual abuse in 2014 said, based on statistics at that time of 1 in 4 girls and 1 in 6 boys being sexually abused in childhood, there were potentially as many as 11.7 million adult survivors in the UK. It is no wonder with figures such as these he openly described sexual abuse in this country as a 'national health epidemic'. It is only since the scandal involving ex-BBC presenter, Jimmy Savile (who died in 2012) came to light, that sexual abuse has become more of an open public discussion. Jimmy Savile was found to have sexually abused numerous children and vulnerable teenagers on a massive scale. In the aftermath of these revelations, survivors who were sexually abused in various institutions, and in some cases by well-known media personalities and other public figures, started to come forward to disclose their experience from decades earlier; hence, the name given to these cases was 'historical sexual abuse'.

Back in 1989 when I disclosed to a neighbourhood friend that my dad was sexually abusing me, I thought I was the only person going through it. Twenty years later, I found out that two other girls in my class at that time were also experiencing sexual abuse. Apart from that life-saving school campaign run by Childline in the late eighties, there were no adverts on the radio or TV that highlighted sexual abuse, and no one mentioned or talked about it – well at least not openly. In fact, the eighties seemed like such an innocent decade. All seemed normal from the outside looking in, but with revelations from popular child actors from the eighties –Corey Feldman and *Diff'rent Strokes* actor, Todd Bridges – about the sexual abuse they experienced on shows, it was far from the innocent decade it seemed.

Looking back at TV programmes and music from that era, sex was subliminally displayed in plain sight – not upfront in your face like in society today. Pop songs back then appeared playful and innocent in nature…well apart from music by artists such as Prince and Madonna, who penned overtly sexual songs. This was as close as anything I ever saw in relation to sex being mentioned, and even then, my comprehension of what they were singing about was non-existent.

It was a couple of weeks after the Childline visit to my school that I made my disclosure to a friend. To finally be able to tell someone what was happening to me was a huge relief. I had dreamt of this day for so long and thought as soon as I named 'it', all of a sudden I would be free from its grasp and that somehow, I would transform back to the playful, joyful girl I was before it happened. But the reality was very different to what I had imagined.

THE VICTIM EXPERIENCE – AFTER DISCLOSURE

If I am being honest, I did not expect the police or social services to act so quickly on my disclosure, let alone come to my house. I did not expect my friend to tell anyone what was happening to me but I am glad she felt led to act. I was taken upstairs to my bedroom and questioned by two social workers from Wandsworth children services who arrived at my house with the police. After the discussion, one of the social workers promptly told me to pack some belongings into plastic bags and explained I would be placed in an emergency foster care placement.

I was scared to be in such unfamiliar surroundings but at the same time relieved that my dad could no longer touch me in any way. I had to undergo a physical examination at St Thomas' Hospital and I was interviewed at a special suite for children at Barnes Police Station in Putney, London. My interview was video recorded and analysed by professionals from behind a mirrored window. I was seen by a psychologist within my first week in care and she diagnosed me as suffering from PTSD (Post Traumatic Stress Disorder). I was only 13 years old and I found the whole initial process traumatising. I never opened up to anyone before and had trouble doing so, but I had a lovely social worker called Ionia who supported me through it.

My treatment by the police and other authorities as a young traumatised girl was positive considering the seriousness of the situation. But my experience with my parents was totally different. I was treated like the perpetrator of my own abuse. Mum accused me of being an attention seeking drama queen, whilst my dad was treated like the victim.

This is a scenario familiar to many survivors I have had discussions with and is a common thread that intertwines and connects throughout each of our individual experiences – friends I had whilst in government care, brief conversations I have had with strangers, women and men I have supported through the work of Daughter Arise. Some survivors shared that when they found the strength and courage to speak out, they were treated as an outcast for daring to voice the unimaginable. Instead of being listened to or supported, they were treated as the person who had committed the crime, when in fact the crime had been committed against them. The fact that sexual abuse has and is still happening is an outrage in itself. In the majority of cases, the burden of blame and responsibility – whether that is placing the burden on the survivor to keep the abuse secret or the decision to shield the perpetrator from the responsibility of their actions – predominately always falls on the shoulders of the survivor of abuse.

SPEAKING OUT – THE OBSTACLES

There are many reasons why survivors of sexual abuse do not speak out sooner. Fear, guilt, shame, threats of violence by the abuser, or consequences threatened by family; loss of family and friendships, humiliation, rejection or as many victims are told, 'no one will believe you', are some of the factors that can affect the decision to speak out. When added to the unresolved hopelessness the survivor may already feel about the situation, these feelings and threats only serve as a reminder of the powerlessness felt since their abuse. Sexual abuse may not carry signs of physical violence but as researcher and philosopher, Gloria Origgi, stated at the 'right to be believed' forum event, 'The psychological violence in the case of sexual abuse is much worse'. I have supported survivors through the disclosure process and have witnessed loved one's reactions to the news. Comments such as, 'If this really happened, why not say something sooner?' are commonly given as the basis for not believing their disclosure. If only it was that simple. The issue of disclosing sexual abuse is not as clear-cut as black and white. The complexities of sexual abuse are as difficult to address now as they have ever been because of the different internal and external dynamics concerning the survivor's personal circumstances.

This is never taken into societal consideration in regards to why survivors do not immediately disclose sexual abuse. Many people think physical signs of injury are the pinnacle proof of evidence that a crime has taken place. In most cases, sexual abuse leaves no physical evidence but its devastation comes in other ways. When you have experienced sexual abuse, it affects you in ways you do not even realise, sometimes years after the event. Memories of pain and betrayal may ease with time but the violation of its intrusiveness, the shackle of shame and guilt that invites itself into your life and cuffs onto you as a burden to remind you of its presence is something many survivors find hard to break free from until this day.

Regardless of physical evidence, the trauma left behind can only be expressed by the one wronged by its cruel injustice. To suffer the pain of being robbed of your innocence and have it hinder your right to live life to the full is a travesty. Through each of our own individual stories, the power of personal testimony is the only thing millions of us have in a world that still cannot fathom the wounds caused by a crime many of us will never see justice for.

On the subject of personal testimony, Gloria Origgi commented, 'There is always an emotional cost for the person'. The question, she said, that must be asked when considering the testimony of someone is, 'What interest does it serve for the person to speak out?' This question should seriously be considered. No survivor who has been through sexual abuse would willingly speak out and put themselves through the torment of having their character picked apart or having their life as they know it turned upside down if it were not true. The right to be believed, it seems in the case of a survivor of sexual abuse, has to be earned; to convince others it happened. It is the only crime where in most cases the 'your word against mine' approach is played out in a courtroom. In most circumstances, the former (earning the right to be believed) seems to apply to the survivor of sexual abuse whether in going to the police, getting justice in court or telling family or friends.

I could have kept quiet, yet when presented with the opportunity to tell someone, I chose to because I sensed something greater was at risk of being destroyed within me. It was in my interest to tell someone because I was in danger from that family. I have never wavered from telling the truth about my story nor shirked away from telling the brutality and havoc it caused in my life. When sharing my experience with different audiences over the years as an inspirational speaker, I always say that if God would have shown me the cost – emotional pain, hardship and the many years it would take in order to be free from the effects of being abused – and given me the opportunity to go back in time to make a different choice, I still would have chosen to speak out; I still would have made the same decision.

It may seem like a no-win situation in taking the decision to speak out, but the person who will benefit the most from doing so is you. It is about you being able to start to come to terms with your past so that you can start to heal. There are no two ways around it: in order to be free from your past it must be acknowledged and addressed; only then can you make choices not tainted or influenced by past trauma, and look towards the future with a different perspective.

18

In an ideal situation, I would have welcomed support from my family but unfortunately, this was not the case. Whilst it is understandable that shock is a natural emotional reaction to the disclosure of sexual abuse, it can also cause family and friends to close ranks and go into denial. A negative reaction can leave the survivor feeling devastated and compound the guilt and shame further. On speaking out, I was painted as a jealous troublemaker unable to adhere to family rules and boundaries; yet in full view of my mum, my dad was able to come into the bathroom night after night whilst I had my wash. Never once was her suspicion triggered by his actions. My family closed ranks, and helped my dad discard evidence whilst he played the victim of a malicious lie in spite of factual documented evidence.

GIVING THE CHILD A VOICE

It is easy to believe because of a child's stature and emotional immaturity that they would lie about someone sexually abusing them. An adult can equate these factors to believe the child is mistaken. The societal mindset is subconsciously programmed with the standard belief that an adult is automatically a person of truth whilst the child is capable of making up lies. How as a child do you articulate something as confusing and horrifying as sexual abuse? Maybe you were in this position. Did you know it was wrong? Did you have the vocabulary or understanding to express what was happening to you?

It is rare for a child to outright tell someone they are being sexually abused. For some children that manage to speak out, their disclosure is often awkward or expressed in an innocent way. Other children express distress in other ways: being withdrawn, showing fear or hesitance around a certain person, using sexually explicit language or showing angry and aggressive behaviour can all be clues that something is wrong. In whatever form these indicators reveal themselves, this should alert the caregiver/adult to investigate further. If the child is not exposed to this behaviour under your care, the question should be where is the child getting this information or behaviour from?

The perpetrator of the abuse relies on the fact they are in a position of power, trust, authority or good standing with those around the child to go undetected in manipulating the child into a position to abuse.

The perpetrator can quite easily cover their tracks, especially if they are well liked and respected in the family and community. This is why if you have children, it is important to:

- Teach them about their bodies and correct names for their body parts rather than given them little cutes names (flower, winkle, etc.). This will help make a difference in them being able to articulate if someone touches them in the wrong way.
- If you have children, tell them they are valuable, important and special – that no has the right to do what they want to them. Teach your child their body is their own.
- Develop a good relationship with your child by spending time with them. Open communication will help your child to open up to you if something is wrong.
- Teach your child the difference between good and bad secrets.What is a good secret? A surprise birthday party or gifts for a loved one, for instance. Tell them the outcome of the secret. Personally, I do not encourage secrets. As someone who grew up in an extremely secretive family, I have learned that the darkness of secrecy allowed destructive and unhealthy situations to breed. I have taught both of my daughters, especially my youngest daughter who is now 12 years old, that if anyone encourages her to keep secrets in any form she should tell me. I find it totally inappropriate for an adult or someone older to choose to have this type of communication with a child.

THE PERPETRATOR

The perpetrator of abuse in most cases gravitates to children who are in dysfunctional or vulnerable situations. For the abuser, sexual abuse is not about sex but about power and control. It is important to note that a person with this intention has to make a deliberate decision to act on their desire; they do not just stumble into doing it. In his research paper called, 'The Four Preconditions Model', Professor David Finkelhor, a leading sociologist known for his research into child sexual abuse describes his theory that there is a four stage process the individual must go through in order to proceed to the final act of sexually abusing a child:

- **Motivation to abuse:** desire to abuse;
- **Overcome internal inhibitions:** there are individuals who find the idea of sexual encounters with children arousing but they do not act on it, because inhibitions prevent them from doing so. This must be overcome in order to abuse the child.
- **Overcome external inhibitions:** once internal inhibitions have been overcome, the individual must create or establish situations where abuse can occur.
- **Overcome resistance of child:** use of bribes, gifts or threats.

Professor David Finkelhor states that interruption of this process (meaning if all four stages have not been passed through) will prevent the abusive act. If all four stages have been passed, the perpetrator will look for opportunities and situations to exploit and abuse their victim.

The abuser is always careful not to show their true intentions towards the child and will never intentionally expose themselves. Just as many survivors have learned to wear a mask of normalcy in front of others to cope with everyday life, the perpetrator of abuse wears a mask of normality and decency in front of people to hide their destructive nature. The façade they portray in front of other people is only let down when they seize the opportunity to corner their victim – it is then their true intentions are revealed. This is one of the main reasons why people find it hard to believe when a member of the family or community is accused of such an act, because of how the person presents in public. An example of this is in the case of Rolf Harris, a celebrity who was famous during the eighties for various TV shows. The shock and denial displayed by some members of the public when he was found guilty of committing acts of sexual abuse were quite sad to see. I saw Facebook posts of people lamenting what a shame it was, blaming the victims and how they could not believe he would do such a thing. People could not reconcile the man in court convicted of these shameful crimes with the entertainer they watched on TV – the quirky old man with a love of art, drawing and acting silly. However, to his victims he was a calculating sexual predator.

It is important that we observe and listen to our children. We must educate ourselves not only as parents and caregivers but as members of society who have a duty to protect the most vulnerable amongst us. We need to familiarise ourselves with the signs that a child is at risk of being sexually abused, and be proactive in safeguarding our children against possible dangers. More often than not, there are indicators present that act as warnings that a child is being abused.

SEXUAL ABUSE INDICATORS

Whilst writing my autobiography, 'Daughter Arise', and from the knowledge I have learned from educating myself about sexual abuse over the years, I clearly saw from my own experience that warning signs were present in my behaviour during childhood that indicated I was being sexually abused.

My indicators were:
- Depression;
- Lying;
- Stealing;
- Going to bed at earlier times than set;
- Mood swings (withdrawn, angry, hyperactive);
- Sexualised behaviour;
- Secretiveness;
- Suicide attempts – (cries for help);
- Attempts to express to Mum something was going on;
- Confectionary, monetary gifts and favouritism by Dad (siblings left out);

If that was not enough to set alarm bells ringing, my dad wanted to leave my mum when I was 10 years old and only wanted to take me with him – not, my brother or sister. It was only when he asked me to go and I said no, thinking I would finally be free of him that he decided to stay. The abuse then continued for another three years.

Other indicators that a child may be exposed to sexual abuse are:

- Bed wetting;
- Self-harm;
- Soreness or redness in the genital/anal area;
- STD (sexually transmitted diseases);
- Clingy behaviour;
- Fear or hesitancy around a particular person;
- Inappropriate sexualised behaviour or language;
- Nightmares or bad dreams;
- Asking probing scenario questions around abuse.

The list is not exhaustive. Maybe looking back on your childhood, you recognise indicators that were present for you but unfortunately were either ignored or not picked up by those around you. It is not your fault. As children, we can only express ourselves to the best of our ability with vocabulary and information we had then, and if we did not have that or even know what was happening to us was wrong then it would be very difficult to articulate.

It is a shame no one heard or saw your cry for help or maybe you kept quiet because you were scared. You may never have had a voice in the past but you are now choosing to start the process of having one by getting this book. You are taking action for your future by choosing to empower yourself by facing what has happened to you. Your experience need not be in vain; one day, in your own unique way, you may able to let others know they do not have to suffer alone.

AWARENESS

At the Daughter Arise afternoon tea awareness event held in 2014, one of our guest speakers shared her account of finding out her 3-year-old daughter was being sexually abused by her husband from whom she was separated. Her daughter could not articulate what was going on, but her sexualised behaviour – masturbation and dry humping – alerted her mother that something was wrong because she had some knowledge of sexual abuse indicators through her work, even though no physical signs were present. In a caring and loving manner she gently asked her daughter where she learned to do the things she was doing, and in a totally innocent way her daughter told her this was what her daddy taught her to do. Fortunately for this child, because she had the support, love and help of her mother and other key people to help her, she is on the road to recovery. It was quite upsetting to hear this story and I fully commend this parent's honesty and bravery in voicing such a painful and heartbreaking experience in a public arena, to give her daughter a voice and to help educate others.

Many survivors of sexual abuse grow up and never disclose to anyone what has happened to them. The question the government should be asking is what is happening to these victims/survivors once they reach past the threshold age of being a child? Who is helping them to come to terms with the trauma they endured from sexual abuse? This information is not hard to find out, and as the government has at their disposal statisticians, advisers and research resources, I believe the hesitancy in dealing effectively with this huge scale problem is down to money, because in order to provide what is needed to support survivors will involve financial investment first (for resources, people and buildings). On ground level, it is small support organisations such as Daughter Arise or charities such as NAPAC (National Association of People Abused in Childhood) who are trying to help support survivors to rebuild their lives.

Helping survivors is done, it seems, as a poor after thought; a knee jerk reaction to problems that come up for them. Institutions, such as prisons and mental health hospitals, are home to hundreds of people whose root issues stemmed from being abused – especially sexually abused – in childhood. This is not including those who have turned to drugs, prostitution, living homeless, in the care system or those struggling with a range of life-changing issues that stem from this trauma. Their need to be local and national forums and events on sexual abuse for it to be discussed and addressed openly and consistently, and it should by either spearheaded or in conjunction with the government – instead of relying on survivors or community organisations to do the core work themselves.

In Lambeth where I live, there is a need for this and I have tried to provide this through the organisation Daughter Arise. A safe environment is needed where those affected, professionals in the field, local Councillors or MPs, and other supporters can come together to discuss this issue in a non-condemning atmosphere to explore ideas and solutions.

The harsh reality is, many adult survivors are left to deal with their issues by themselves, for society seems to show little care. Struggling in silence with mental health and emotional issues can affect everyday life but this has been normal for many survivors. Specialised counselling for sexual abuse is expensive and is not provided on the National Health Service; what is offered instead is generalised one-size-fits-all counselling. At a minimum of fifty pounds a time for each session, the amount of sessions it would take to get to a stage to open up enough to talk to the counsellor is costly because it takes time to build trust. I believe the government should invest in opening specialised support centres so that survivors can access affordable and appropriate counselling; but also create an empowering environment, such as support groups for survivors to connect with one another.

These ideas may seem far-fetched but I have seen the promise of them in action. What I found wonderful about creating the afternoon tea events that Daughter Arise hosted was the sense of community that was established in such a short time. I fundraised, organised and executed these empowering events with a team of volunteers. Survivors of abuse and supporters of the cause from all over the country came together to talk, ask questions, openly communicate and share experiences and explore solutions. By providing a safe inclusive environment, for the first time some survivors felt supported and encouraged to share their voice. After the event, when I read the feedback forms, it is evident that many people do not know what indicators of sexual abuse are, and do not know how to talk to their children about bodily boundaries or how sexual abuse affects lives in the aftermath – especially in adult survivors. This is why continued awareness is important.

With the information presented by NAPAC (National Association of Children Abused in Childhood), one of the organisations I invited to speak at the event, and the personal stories shared by the survivors that support Daughter Arise, it gave fellow adult survivors space to reflect on how their experience impacted on their lives. MOSAC (Mother of Sexually Abused Children) educated parents and caregivers at the event on how to talk to children about their bodies and indicators of possible sexual abuse.

Education is key in helping people to understand what sexual abuse is and crucial in breaking down the stigma, shame and societal attitude surrounding it. By whatever means, we need to share this information in a way that people can understand, and it is important to address this as we see the rise of peer sexual abuse – children sexually abusing other children (*some reports state a 71% increase in this problem, especially in schools*). There are many factors that play a part in why there has been a huge rise. In my opinion, the internet, the breakdown in family structure, lack of parenting and children not being taught boundaries, access to porn and other sexually disturbing images are all part of the problem, but more research needs to explore the reasons why.

Whilst raising awareness will help reduce the incidences of sexual abuse, it will not eradicate the problem altogether; but at the very least it will help future generations of children find the vocabulary to voice it should it happen to them, and hopefully help people to have a better understanding of this problem.

SEXUAL ABUSE, THE LAW AND JUSTICE

I attended a European philosophy debate event at the forum, London School of Economics called 'a right to be believed'. It sought to open a dialogue to explore why, in terms of sexual abuse cases, offences have frequently gone unpunished because victims have not been believed; and how, if at all, personal testimony can be reconciled with the law and principle of innocent until proven guilty. The panel was made up of three experts in their respective fields: Gloria Origgi (Researcher and Philosopher, Institute Jean Nicod CNRS, Paris – knowledgeable in personal testimony research); Louise Ellison (Professor of Law, University of Leeds); and Stephen Vullo (QC, Criminal Barrister).

I was interested in going to this debate for a number of reasons: firstly, because I was sexually abused as a child and had partially gone through the legal process. Secondly, as a woman who believes strongly in the power of personal testimony, who publicly shares my story to educate and empower others. Lastly, as a leader of an organisation that predominately deals with survivors of what the law classifies as 'historical sexual abuse', I wanted to know how the law deals with cases of past abuse and to hear specifically if the prosecution rate is successful.

As I listened, I found myself reflecting on my past experience and I wondered, in the context and criteria of the law as it stands today, if I were to decide as an 'historical sexual abuse victim' to go back and report it to the police now, would my case be treated differently than it was twenty-seven years ago?

The police, doctors, psychologist and social workers in my case did indeed believe my account of events (I have the documented reports). The problem, however, arose from the Crown Prosecution Service who said that, whilst there was conclusive physical evidence of actual sexual abuse, because the room where most of the incidents took place (the room over at gran's house) was cleared out (by my dad, gran and mum) they were not confident that physical evidence alone was enough to secure a conviction, so my dad was not taken to court. It was not easy for me to articulate in detail the things he did to me and for a long time, it felt like what I went through counted for nothing. The experience left me angry and disappointed; I felt like I had done something wrong, when in fact I was the victim.

Before the mid-nineties, just twenty years ago, QC Barrister Stephen Vullo said the police worked from a standpoint of disbelieving victims first, making the assumption that children were liars, especially unbelievable in matters such as abuse. He explained massive changes have taken place over the last twenty years in how cases of this nature are approached and prosecuted. The introduction of special measures under the provision of The Victim Charter (video interviews, etc.) are meant to support victims going through the legal process; however, it seems survivors are not quite benefitting from these changes as they should.

The decision to report sexual abuse to the legal authorities is a decision that is not taken lightly. For the brave minority of victims who have found the courage to go to the police in the first place, the process is an emotionally draining and extremely difficult one that needs to be handled with the sensitivity it respectively deserves; because to treat the disclosure with disdain will only compound an already traumatising experience. Evidence and research carried out by the HM inspectorate constabulary stated that, while in theory police are supposed to be recording reported allegations of sexual abuse – working from guidelines set by their directorate; working from the assumption that allegations reported are true (accepting what victims say in the first instance then carrying out a thorough fact finding investigation to find 'evidence of truth') – in practice, constabularies across the country are not doing this consistently, and shockingly their findings state that since the Jimmy Savile scandal, this has not really changed. It is so serious that the HM inspectorate highlighted this 'as an area of grave concern'.

How is this so? With all the press coverage, panels and documentaries that have pulled apart, legally and morally, every aspect of how this man – a prominent face of a national institution such as the BBC – was able to commit sexual abuse of this magnitude, how have the attitudes and practices of the police not really changed? Has the shock of this scandal not finally awoken the government and authorities to the seriousness and scale of this health epidemic?

In my opinion not only should lessons be learned from Jimmy Savile and other sexual abuse scandals, they should be used as an opportunity to gain a deeper understanding of the issues and challenges that affect why victims do not immediately come forward in the first place. These cases should be used to continuously review obstacles that hinder the administration of justice. Is it possible this information could be used as a resource to help those responsible for administering the law gain better insight? I believe it is worth considering, especially when we hear of court cases where victims have to choose between getting therapeutic help and support first or pursuing the legal process; or cases when faulty video and recording equipment has failed to work for victims during interviews, as claimed by Professor Louise Ellison, an advocate for the vulnerable going through the law system. Surely emotional and psychological support is most needed when going through something as traumatic as this. The fact is, many victims already feel they will not be believed and this is one of the major reasons why they do not come forward. Any support to help those wronged pursue justice should be encouraged. If survivors of this crime do not feel supported during and through the criminal process, the likelihood is they will not see it through to the end. This will mean the perpetrator escapes being held accountable for his or her actions and becomes a risk to another child.

28

Jimmy Savile died without being held accountable for his crimes and the survivors were the ones left to pick up the pieces of their lives. But it is not only famous and powerful people who are not being held accountable for their actions of sexual abuse – every day, in families and communities all over the world others who perpetrate these offences are getting away with it too.

In the face of these findings, and with the slow realisation of the impact of sexual abuse, I wonder what will bring about the drastic change needed to take the huge burden of responsibility off the victim/survivor to enable them to feel confident in speaking out without the fear of being treated like the perpetrator of their own abuse.

There are no guarantees in the outcome of reporting sexual abuse to the police but nevertheless it should be reported because it is a crime. The government should use their authoritative influence as leaders on a national scale to encourage victims to report it and make it known that it will be taken seriously. I still do not see any high impacting media messages or government led initiatives highlighting the seriousness of sexual abuse or the implications it can have in the aftermath. I believe the reason is because of money. Money is what funds resources, campaigns and initiatives and the lack of it has an effect on all services (police, courts, mental health support). I also believe it is highly likely that unless there are other complainants of the abuser, physical or documented evidence that backs the timeline in favour of the victim, it will rest solely on their personal testimony. The odds of the perpetrator of abuse getting a custodial sentence (if it even makes it to court) are not favourable; the prosecution rate for sexual abuse cases is below 50%.

I personally know of cases where the survivor has reported their experience that happened many years ago (that has been classed as an historical case) to the police, and gone through the court process, only to see the abuser found not guilty. Instead, the offence is recorded against their name for future reference – in case an allegation comes up against them again, it will show they have been taken to court previously for a similar offence. Other survivors (I know of two cases) have seen the abuser receive a substantial sentence because, as the police have gone back in their family history as part of the investigation, they have found other victims that have had a similar experience at the hands of the perpetrator. Some survivors withdraw from the court process because of the stress, and it is no surprise when you learn it can take up to two years for the case to be heard in court; that is a long time.

The personal obstacles a survivor has to overcome in order to get to a point of acknowledging and disclosing, in most circumstances, takes place years after the abuse – as we have seen in cases such as Savile. Statistics and documented research from experts respected in the field of sexual abuse, and survivors I have supported through Daughter Arise, corroborate this as truth. Some survivors never tell anyone and live with the burden of it.

The law quite rightly is there to be fair and unbiased; many would argue this is not the case. The law cannot operate from being led by human emotions because if it were based on feelings, the system would never work. It has to operate from a standard of guidelines and framework to administer justice, and because of that it is possible for people to slip through the net or not be given the sentences we think they deserve. The people behind the roles, in police organisations or bar councils, would benefit from inviting reputable people or organisations to run courses for their employees on sexual abuse awareness to gain more of an understanding into how it affects the survivor. As the saying goes, knowledge is power.

At the 'a right to be believed' forum, the questions I had were neither addressed (I did try and put up my hand a few times but I was not picked during the debate) or asked by any of the audience members, who were mainly law students interested in legal complexities of such cases rather than the emotional dilemmas facing the victim going through the process. It would have been interesting to know from the legal experts on the panel what is taken into consideration when forming a historical sexual abuse prosecution case and how the police come to a conclusion of charging someone accused of it where no physical evidence is present.

So, on the basis of what I heard, would I choose to go back and report to the police again now, and go through the legal process to pursue justice? Sometimes I think I should, more for principle rather than anything else. But as someone who has a relationship with Jesus Christ, I rest assured that the ultimate justice will be served through him, and my dad will eventually answer for what he did to

30

me. From the assurance of God's word (the bible) he will not go unpunished (*vengeance is mine says the Lord, he will repay – Romans 12:19*). I have gained peace and comfort over the years from knowing this. My dad is in his later years of life now; my gran has passed away and I have not allowed their actions to define me. It has taken a lot for me to recover from what was done to me, and in the last decade I have slowly broken out from the shadow of its devastation. I have chosen to move on, and whilst the faint memory of disappointment lingers from time to time because of injustice, I choose to use my experiences to help others pursue freedom and justice instead.

INDEPENDENT INQUIRY INTO CHILD SEXUAL ABUSE

On the 7th July 2014, Theresa May, who was then Home Secretary, announced that an independent inquiry would be established to examine how the countries' institutions (in UK) handled their duty of care to protect children from sexual abuse in England and Wales. The inquiry (now named The Independent Inquiry into Child Sexual Abuse) was set up after the scale of sexual abuse committed by Jimmy Savile was exposed. The inquiry proceeded on 8th July 2014, but in the months following its set up it has been problematic in places and suffered many setbacks, including the resignation of three chairpersons and the survivor group SOSA (Survivors of Organised and Institutional Abuse) declaring in June 2017 that the 'inquiry was not fit for purpose'. By the time the third chair, Dame Goddard, was appointed, it seemed that at last ground-breaking progress would be made in this inquiry. She announced separate investigations would be undertaken that included Members of Parliament (MPs), local council, and church organisations. Information concerning sexual abuse in institutions dating back years was handed to the police to investigate as they came to light. It seemed to be going in the right direction but unfortunately, the panel was disbanded and Dame Goddard resigned. A new panel was set up with Professor Alexis Jay as the new chairman – now the fourth in succession.

In my opinion, thus far, there seems to be an unknown force operating in the background to hinder this inquiry. Remember the nature of this inquiry is to investigate not only establishment abuse but those in high-level positions of authority that have used their power and privilege to sexually abuse vulnerable children. It is not going to be easy to uncover; as we have seen so far, those that held high profile positions (Cyril Smith, Savile) were allowed to pass away with no accountability for their crimes, but this inquiry must prevail and the truth must come to light. If this panel succeeds in the purpose for which it was established, it could bring a real chance for drastic change, not only in the way institutions and organisations handle sexual abuse allegations and reporting, but also in breaking down some of the misconceptions and stereotypes surrounding survivors of sexual abuse and the way they're perceived. I believe, to an extent, if this inquiry is successful it can help empower victims and survivors, by giving them confidence that their voice will be heard.

THE TRUTH PROJECT

The Truth Project was set up as part of the Independent Inquiry into Child Sexual Abuse. It is one of three strands that form the inquiry; public hearings and research and analysis are the other components. Information collated from all three strands will make up the final recommendations of the inquiry. The aim of The Truth Project is to give survivors of childhood sexual abuse a chance for their voices to be heard by sharing their experiences and allowing the inquiry to learn from the past to build a better future for victims and survivors, and to make recommendations that will protect children from risk of abuse.

I took part in The Truth Project. I initially contacted them by phone in March 2018 after reading online in a news article about their work, and from reading both positive and negative comments from those who took part and those who supported someone else in participating. The project support representative clearly explained the process to me and I was sent information and a consent form to complete. Survivors who take part in the project can share their experience by phone, audio recording, private face-to-face session, in writing or may even choose to share drawings or creative writing. I chose the private face-to-face session.

I attended my session in May 2018. I was not nervous leading up to the day but on the day, I did feel slightly anxious as I did not know what to expect. But as I sat with the support worker who had contacted me to offer support leading up to this day, it was clear this was just about me sharing my experience; nothing more or less.

I was given up to an hour and half to do this, with the option to book time to come back. That was what I found positive about The Truth Project; it took into account the feelings of the survivor, offering different ways for the individual to share their experience. The way in which they explained what it would entail was clear: the process, the possible ramifications of naming the perpetrator (they explained if named they have a duty to report to the police) and their duty of care.

Two professionals, both ladies that worked on behalf of The Truth Project held the session. One was a trained counsellor with a background in working with sexual abuse victims/survivors and the other, a note taker who went through the legalities and asked for my consent, took notes and recorded the interview. The session went as well as expected under the circumstances. It never gets easier to talk about the details of what happened to me as a child. I cried and it made me feel vulnerable, but it didn't make me regress back to a place of feeling helpless or hopeless. Even though it was emotionally tough, I felt empowered by being part of the process. The counsellor was there to listen and at times asked for clarification of information I shared where needed. The session was led in a gentle manner and I was in control of how and what I shared; I never felt pressurised in any way.

After the session, the support worker who called me in the weeks before, sat and made sure I was okay before I left and explained that for up to six weeks I would be able to have phone support if I needed it. I would say this is the only negative I felt about The Truth Project – there was no after support as promised. I did not receive any phone call or email, checking if I was okay after disclosing something so difficult. Fortunately for me, I have access to support through a counsellor but for those who don't have this, it could prove detrimental to them as opening up about something so traumatic could trigger very negative feelings and flashbacks. The after support needs to be more robust because if they do not offer the full service they stated at the beginning, it could ruin their credibility with victims/survivors and will make it more difficult for potential survivors to come forward, especially since trust and truth is the foundation on which they are building this project.

Out of interest I read their first interim report that was released in October 2017 in relation to their first year, June 2016–June 2017. One of the key things that stuck out for me in terms of the statistics regarding participation of the BME (Black, Minority, Ethnic) communities is that survivors from these backgrounds are not participating in the project. Out of the 249 private face-to-face sessions held June 2016–June 2017, only 7% of those were from the BME communities. These statistics seem to back up information shared from survivors that Daughter Arise has supported over the years and information reported from these groups – that sexual abuse is tolerated and accepted in these communities and to speak out is not an acceptable thing to do. For those who have bravely done so, they are pressurised to deny it happened, shunned and looked down upon for telling their truth.

The Truth Project has stated they are currently developing a plan to increase participation from Black, Minority and Ethnic communities. It will be interesting to see how they will engage with these communities, as a conditioned mindset and generational acceptability has become the norm towards sexual abuse in a large majority of families. Unfortunately, secrecy and shame are more acceptable to the majority rather than allowing outsiders to bring disrepute on the family name.

SEXUAL ABUSE – HOW SERIOUS IS IT?

In my opinion, sexual abuse is not treated with the seriousness it deserves, especially for something described as a 'national health epidemic'. Think of the Ebola virus or, many years ago in the U.K, mad cow disease. The way these epidemics were constantly highlighted in the news left an impression they were to be treated very seriously. The information given on the news told you where it came from, symptoms to look out for, and you were warned of the dangers of leaving symptoms unchecked, and warned that if you even suspected having it to contact the relevant authorities immediately, highlighting the possible consequence if ignored. The urgency of these health epidemics came and went but I still remember the news surrounding them to this day.

Sexual abuse is affecting the mental, emotional, physical health and quality of life of millions of victims and survivors all over the world in one form or another; yet it does not get half the media coverage that these health scares had. The public needs to be bombarded with the message of the dangers of sexual abuse, to be made aware this is not a harmless or victimless crime – it has real life consequences; even fatal.

An insight from a report published on the scale of problems caused by sexual abuse by the World Health Organisation 2016 (based on research from 39 countries) shows:

- Women who have been physically or sexually abused have higher rates of mental ill health, unintended pregnancies, abortions and miscarriages than non-abused women;
- Girls are far more likely than boys to suffer sexual abuse;
- International studies reveal that a quarter of all adults have been physically abused as a child and 1 in 5 women and 1 in 13 men report having been sexually abused as children;
- 800 million people worldwide have experienced childhood sexual abuse, with over 500 million having experienced contact or intercourse types of abuse;
- CSA (childhood sexual abuse) is not only common, it is also damaging. Research conducted in economically industrialised countries has shown CSA increases the risk of a range of mental disorders in later life, including depression, panic disorders, alcohol and drug abuse and dependence, post-traumatic stress disorder and suicide;
- Risks increase with the intrusiveness of the abuse;
- Uncertainty remains because of the lack of knowledge about the impact of cultural differences on CSA prevalence and its relationship with mental disorders. It is, however, certain that CSA causes considerable burden of disease. It is estimated that about 33% of post-traumatic stress disorder in females and 21% in males is attributable to CSA. The attributed fraction for panic disorders is 11% worldwide, and CSA is estimated to cause 5-8% of self-inflicted injuries, unipolar depression and alcohol and drug use disorders. Overall, 0.1% of deaths worldwide (79,000) were attributable to CSA.

These statistics are shocking and heart breaking and show the true extent to which sexual abuse affects lives. Help should be readily at hand for those who need it; but I know this is not always the case, as in some parts of the world sexual abuse is not even recognised let alone addressed as an issue people need help with, and many victims and survivors don't even realise that difficult shameful thing that happened to them was sexual abuse. It is startling that 79,000 people's deaths were caused directly by sexual abuse, and I wonder what difference compassion, understanding and support could have made in those lives; one life lost is one life too many.

CULTURAL ATTITUDES AND PERCEPTIONS TOWARDS SEXUAL ABUSE IN THE BLACK MINORITY COMMUNITY

Generational sexual abuse and incest are common within many communities worldwide and accepted as a normal way of life. As mentioned in the segment titled 'The Truth Project' where I talk about the shocking statistics regarding the lack of participation from victims and survivors from black ethnic communities, I believe this is one of the main reasons why individuals from these groups do not disclose. Protecting the abuser whilst vilifying the victim is a common problem within Caribbean and African communities; although this enabling behaviour is not confined to these groups – it is a worldwide problem faced by victims and survivors of all races.

This was certainly the case in regards to my birth family, and I experienced first-hand the effect and repercussions of being in such a situation. As a black woman that originates from a background that descends from Jamaican heritage, and as a survivor of incest from this community, I want to briefly address this issue from this standpoint. I know many women and men from these communities that have been crushed by their treatment at the hands of their family and social community.

Denial of sexual abuse and enabling the abuser is a common problem that has never been widely addressed in the black community. There is a common saying amongst our people: 'what goes on in your house, should stay in your house' – that even applies to the crime of sexual abuse; family problems should not be discussed

36

with outsiders. This mindset of dealing with difficult issues, not just sexual abuse, is ingrained, passed down the family generations that believe if you ignore the problem and sweep it under the proverbial carpet, it will go away. Relatives, friends or other members of the victim's social circle, in many cases know sexual abuse is going on. There have been incidents where a family member has walked in on the perpetrator in action but rather than report it to the appropriate authorities, chosen to ignore it.

In my autobiography, 'Daughter Arise', I spoke of a conversation I had with my mum years after my own abuse about the times my dad would come into the bathroom night after night when I was a child in full view of her as she sat on her bed watching TV. He would give the reason for assaulting me as he was checking I was washing properly, but in fact he was abusing me. I told her what he was doing during those bathroom visits, thinking she would be upset by the revelation, but instead she replied, 'It is normal for Jamaican fathers to do that to their daughters.'

I was shocked by her response and even asked an older black man whom I respected at the time if he did this to his daughters; he responded no and was shocked that I asked. It was bizarre that she would make such a comment; then it dawned on me that she must have been exposed to this behaviour somewhere in her own life. I found out twenty years later that my dad had initiated a sexual relationship with my mum in her early teens. He was her mum's (my gran's) husband – her stepdad! It all made sense now: the response I got when I tried to tell my mum at 10 years old that I saw my dad and gran naked in bed at her house. At the time my mum called me a liar and my dad beat me for telling the truth. He is a sexual predator that has been protected and enabled by the compliant females within my birth family. According to the Jamaican Vulnerable Communities Coalition, 40% of Jamaicans say their 'first experience of sexual contact was forced and under the age of consent, more often than not perpetrated by someone close to home – a family member, teacher, preacher or community leader'. In the conversations I have had with female survivors of older generations, they confirmed this as their story. With pain in their eyes, they tell of their experience growing up in the Caribbean, being sold out by the very people who were supposed to take care of and protect them as children. Sometimes they were compromised for money; other times for food or education, especially in households that were poor or had many mouths to feed. The family member, friend or acquaintance would expect sexual favours or intercourse as payment for their so-called 'deeds of kindness' and 'help' given to the family. Jamaica has been described by government agencies as 'a nation in the grip of a national sexual abuse epidemic' and human rights groups say 'taboos about reporting incest, rape and the abuse of power by older men are so entrenched that thousands of young girls still continue to suffer in silence'.

This problem was also echoed in findings of a landmark study released by the UNICEF office for Barbados and the Eastern Caribbean, titled 'Perceptions of Attitudes to, and opinions on Child Sexual Abuse in the Eastern Caribbean' (2010). Part of the purpose of the study was to investigate what attitudes people have towards sexual abuse and to identify what situations increase the risk of a child being sexually abused. Even though this research was conducted several years ago, it helped me gain a better insight into why sexual abuse is so hard to address in these communities and why it remains an underreported crime. Two hundred and eighty people participated in the thirty-five focus groups selected from across six countries to take part in this research. The groups were from Anguilla, Barbados, Dominica, Grenada, Montserrat and St Kitts and Nevis and were made up of people from different backgrounds, professionals and practitioners, religious, youth groups, education, employment settings, and mixed in terms of gender, age and socioeconomic status. Also included as an important part of the study were adult survivors of childhood sexual abuse.

Jamaica is not the only island where the sexualisation of children starts early. Children as young as 4 years old are talking and engaging in sexual behaviour in other Caribbean islands too. The focus group in St Kitts and Nevis believed seductive dancing is the gateway to young children being groomed for sexual behaviour. I have witnessed on various YouTube videos young children provocatively dancing in totally inappropriate way. It is no secret that many music artists, especially in the last twenty-five years have promoted, through their music, highly explicit sexual messages. Sexualised music and dancing go hand in hand as part of cultural

38

identity in some Caribbean islands and many adults choose to partake in sexualised dancing in front of their children with little care. In my opinion, I believe certain types of music, which is widely accepted as part of Caribbean dancehall culture, helps to not only promote but also condone sexualised behaviour and lack of boundaries as a normal way of life.

It is not the sole contributor to the issue of sexualisation of children; it is part of the puzzle in the bigger jigsaw of the problem that has helped create the breeding ground for children in these communities to be groomed for sexual abuse. Children need protection from harmful influences, and to be in an environment where this goes on is conditioning the child to think this behaviour is normal. This is dangerous on so many levels and being exposed to this behaviour leaves the child vulnerable to the risk of abuse.

Practitioners interviewed in Barbados cited poor and inadequate sleeping arrangements (many children live with the caregiver in small overcrowded apartments) as environments that lead to children being at risk of exposure to inappropriate sexual behaviour, as many children have to share a bed with the adult or be in the same room where the adults are having sex. Other contributing factors that focus groups believe increased the risk of sexual abuse were mothers having various different relationships with men or what they described as 'boyfriends' who frequent the house, and inadequate parental supervision where mothers who worked nights allowed their partner or family acquaintance to supervise their children. Over half of the respondents (53.6%) believed stepfathers were more likely than biological fathers to sexually abuse children.

Another issue highlighted by all focus groups was the increasing number of adult males in relationships with young girls under the age of consent (aged 16 or under). The views of some of the respondents are interesting. 62.6% did not believe women refusing their partner sex was the reason why men would choose to engage in sexual activity with an underage girl, whilst 17.6% believed this was the reason why. Some even blamed the underage girls by commenting they deliberately seek out these relationships – in some cases citing the mothers as their encouragers to solicit money or gifts from these men in exchange for sex.

As the report was published in 2010, it would be interesting to know how these views would hold up now with the raised awareness in recent years of Child Sexual Exploitation and grooming and if these are acknowledged as forms of sexual abuse and crimes in the Caribbean.

In the UK, the law is of the view that an adult or any groups of individuals that engage in this behaviour are committing a crime. The emphasis is not placed on the child, no matter what circumstance may have led up to them being in the situation.

People have their own perceptions and ideas of what constitutes sexual abuse, and these perceptions have been shaped by the society or environment they have grown up in. This is why the definition set by law is important. It is not okay for an adult to use their position and power to abuse, coerce or manipulate a child into sexual abuse. Free will and the gift of choice has been freely given to everyone by God, and if someone has used their power of choice to abuse you as a child, it is not your fault no matter what anyone says; no child can ever be responsible for the actions of an adult.

The practitioners and professionals that took part in the study had a clear understanding of what was defined as sexual abuse, whilst differing views across the focus groups believed sexual abuse stemmed from the context of the situation, attitude or behaviour rather than what the law states. What constitutes as law ultimately defines sexual abuse of a child. The age of consent in most Caribbean countries is 16 years old – many participants in the focus groups felt this was too young and that the age of consent should be raised to 18 years old.

Social norms and values form part of the framework that influences how law-makers and judges define what a crime is, and this can be reviewed at any time. In my opinion, from reading this report, people are not confident in the ability of the law to handle cases of sexual abuse. This is reflected in the fact that cases are underreported and the records of successful prosecutions are extremely low. A high percentage of people in the focus groups believe confronting the accused and dealing with the disclosure of abuse 'in-house' is the first point of action. I do not believe this tactic is effective because the issues the perpetrator has – which go far beyond their actions – cannot be fixed by a simple telling off. Also, addressing the situation in this manner does not help the victim; it can leave them with little support and in many cases vulnerable to be blamed for the actions of the perpetrator.

Regardless of what may be the perceived outcome, it must be reported. Without reporting it to the relevant authorities, it allows the perpetrator to manipulate the situation and go unaccountable for their actions, allowing them the opportunity to abuse another child.

Great pressure and expectation are always commonly placed on the abused. The influence of community is powerful and if someone who has been abused tries to speak out, pressure is not only applied to them to keep quiet but also in some cases their family. The survivor often has to put aside their own feelings to carry the burden of protecting the reputation of the family and bearing the shame of the abuser. As a global society, we need to continuously challenge these expectations by placing the responsibility back on the abuser and not enabling the abuser by being complicit in silence. From reading this research paper, I began to understand why men like my dad had a mindset to believe it was okay to sexually abuse me, and why women like Mum and Gran enabled him to do so. The fact those older survivors who left Jamaica decades ago comment that they still see the same issues and scenarios repeating themselves with newer generations, shows that much change is needed; but the mentality is deeply ingrained. It is not only damaging to the survivor but little do people realise the damage they cause on each generation of family by choosing to turn a blind eye, and the impact this has on society.

It is common to hear of families where sexual abuse has passed down the generations because it is deeply ingrained. Cultural acceptance, secrecy and enabling, and behaviour left unchallenged has become the 'norm' for the next victim to be groomed for sexual abuse. For instance, the father who rapes and sexually abuses his daughter in these families, rules the household with an iron fist, cultivating an atmosphere of fear, and in doing so thwarts any challenge to his authority or decisions, leaving him free to abuse. He is his own authority and wise in his own eyes; therefore, he does not see his behaviour as wrong, let alone as abuse. Besides intimidation and fear, he may be the main breadwinner or, because of the way of life or family structure tradition (being all the family have ever known, dynamic, behaviour, dos and don'ts passed down the generations), the family members decide to keep quiet about sexual abuse. Herein lays the foundation for enabling and collective denial and acceptance of sexual abuse to be treated as normal. If exposed, the responsibility and blame is put on the victim.

Perpetrators that commit these crimes need to be held accountable by their family and community by reporting it to the police, instead of enabling the abuser by turning a blind eye. In the black community, I have heard people make excuses for male perpetrators of sexual abuse, citing their gender (being a man) as the reason for his lack of self-control, whilst the victim, who is under the age of consent – a child in the eyes of the law – is not afforded any such empathy or sympathy. As mentioned in the UNICEF 2010 report regarding perceptions and attitudes towards sexual abuse, girls and boys from the Caribbean community are accused of being the ones that enticed and led the perpetrator to commit sexual abuse.

In an article I read in the Sunday Observer newspaper (dated April 2012), Dr Sandra Knight, a Paediatric Doctor who works at the Bustamante Hospital in Kingston, Jamaica, spoke of the distress of treating children brought in suffering from horrific injuries caused by sexual abuse. She spoke of the helplessness she feels at seeing some of them succumb to their injuries. Dr Knight has had to treat babies and young children – as young as 3 years old – who have been infected with sexually transmitted diseases such as gonorrhoea and herpes. In the article, a doctor shared an encounter she had with one particular child. The paediatrician gently asked this young girl how she got gonorrhoea, to which the young girl replied, 'My mother tell me na fe tark' ('*My mother told me not to talk about it*' – *patois paraphrased*); even from a young age, secrecy and fear are the weapons used to ensure the next generation keeps the secret.

I have not come across any updated research in relation to this study conducted with focus groups in these regions to evaluate if time has changed their perceptions and attitudes, but I have several friends who have family members in the Caribbean who have said, from conversations with relatives about sexual abuse, little has changed. In fact, they said attitudes are so ingrained that it is now reluctantly seen as a problem that will never change.

I believe things can change but it will take patience, persistence, education, awareness and time to deal with something

42

that has been ingrained for generations. There are several things that could help towards a better understanding of this issue, and it starts from a place of believing prevention is better than cure. Children as young as 5 years old should be given education on their bodies, sexual abuse, boundaries and safe relationships. With the right professionals, this could be done in an age-appropriate way and could help future generations of children who may be experiencing this to tell someone sooner. A wonderful example of an organisation that is doing a great work is Rise Life Management in Jamaica. They work in communities, providing educational, vocational and health-related services for at-risk families. One of the topics they engage with children about is sexual abuse, using interactive workshops.

For the police to have effective and positive engagement with victims of sexual abuse, to encourage them to come forward and build confidence in their ability to be trusted in handling such sensitive matters, they should have survivor-led training. This would give them valuable insight to better understand how sexual abuse affects the victim in the aftermath and how best to support the person through the legal requirements. This training should also be given to the lawyers, barristers and those who work in the law system to help create a better picture of the challenges a victim goes through and to enable a support process through court proceedings.

Another avenue that could possibly help is if organisations that support survivors of childhood sexual abuse could engage with communities through educational workshops and events, with the intention of starting a dialogue, good or bad, to understand the issues and concerns that prevent people speaking out about abuse and reporting it. Raised awareness through media adverts – whether TV or YouTube for example – on child sexual abuse and child sexual exploitation can provide the public with information on this problem. These suggestions are not quick fixes and it will take a long time to undo decades of learned mindset and perceptions in regards to sexual abuse, but these ideas I believe could help to make a start.

Thousands of children worldwide are being sexually abused and because of lack of awareness, resources, education and unwillingness of people within their communities to confront this issue, violation has become an everyday way of life for these children. In countries such as India and Yemen, child rape is rampant: men marrying child brides, high abortion rates, children having children, dying in childbirth or suffering internal bleeding from injuries caused by intercourse, and families where incest produces children born with severe deformities. In South Africa, a myth developed in early 2000 amongst certain adult carriers of HIV that having sex with a virgin (raping a child, babies in some cases) would somehow cleanse them of their disease, resulted in these poor children ending up dead because of their injuries. There are women who have children for the sole purpose of having them raped and killed in Satanic paedophile rings as sacrifices, and not to mention the child sex trade where thousands of children end up missing, sold to the highest bidder for no purpose other than to be used and prostituted for sex. The UK is the most prominent country for children going missing and being sexually exploited; a high percentage goes missing from local authority care.

I share this information with you not to shock or make you uncomfortable but to raise awareness of the depth of which the sickness of sexual abuse runs. It affects all cultures, social classes, religions and faiths and races; it does not discriminate. We hear of the increasing amount of sexual abuse being carried out in all denominations of churches (it is not just a roman catholic church problem); stories of it being exposed has shocked many people, but it is the tip of the iceberg. It is rampant in the most secretive of communities (Jehovah witnesses, Muslim, Jewish and Amish communities) with the isolation of their communities providing the perfect breeding ground for sexual abuse.

It does make for depressing reading all that I have shared so far, but in order to fight this epidemic we need to face the ugliness of it so we can dismantle the myths and address the issues that have caused it to grow at such an alarming rate. Educating people through a range of awareness programmes, preferably delivered most powerfully by courageous survivors willing to share their stories and experience, can help break its demonic secret stronghold and expose it to the light.

Until we as a society can break down the walls of this taboo subject by admitting it goes on far more than we choose to admit and take seriously, it will always be seen as a taboo subject. The stigma and secrecy surrounding it will continue to fan the flames of devastation and destruction.

Jesus Christ paid the price by dying on the cross to expose the works of darkness and restore hope (*'has come to set people free from all that keeps them bound and to expose the works of darkness'* – *Luke 8:17 – paraphrased*). It is the price he had to be pay in order to help those who cannot help themselves and to reconcile people to the living God. In turn, those of us who are willing to have the courage, must stand up against this evil to make a difference. To stand up and be a voice for those experiencing what we suffered, we must understand there will be a cost for us too.

◆ EMPOWER POINT – ONE THING I AM GOING TO DO

All bricks make a house and all small acts of action that we each can do will help towards fighting the evil of child sexual abuse. Write one thing you could do to raise awareness and then do it!

It could be re-tweeting a tweet on the topic if you are on Twitter, posting something on Facebook or supporting organisations like Daughter Arise by letting people know the work we are doing.

QUOTE – THE CONSEQUENCES

'The consequences of childhood sexual abuse reach far and wide. Prisons, mental health hospitals and the cemetery are full of people broken by their experience. Broken hearts, broken lives, broken families equal a broken society. If only the government would care for the impact it has on a person's life, maybe then would they invest more in awareness and education than costly inquiries. Prevention is better than cure. The financial cost to society may be great but the pain caused to the victim is even greater'.

Quote – Yvonne Ellis

NO DREAM

(Poem I wrote in 2000)

It feels like I'm having a bad dream

Like I've left my body, and gone to some dark and frightening place

I can still see myself at 9 years old

When he was naked in the bed

He told me to get on top of him

I was so small and carefree

But from that time my personality left me

Who I thought I was

What I was meant to be, a child

Full of innocence and fun

From that point thereon in

Things were never the same

Still feel his shadow eclipsing my eye sight

The sound of his belt buckle loosening, him taking off his clothes

'Are you getting in the bed?' he'd say

With my back turned to him

My eyes are watering, my mouth is dry

I slowly take off my clothes

With such shame

I see his penis, I'm scared, defenceless

As he lays on top of me

Panting, sweating

I'm not the daughter he raised anymore

But his lover

He forces his tongue in my mouth

I've closed my eyes so tight

That all I can see are different colours

Orange, red and blue

Like every night since

Through the pain and rejection that is left

I open my eyes to realise

It is not a dream

I am awake

He is down between my legs now

He is still there

Through my depression and medication, I open my eyes

Every morning

It is not a dream

Everything is exactly how it has always been

Not a dream

Awake in a nightmare

I am still here

Yvonne

MY INNER BATTLE - HOW I FELT POST ABUSE

Worthless Unloveable Inferior Undeserving of anything good

Isolated Used Crazy Voiceless

Suicidal Scared Abandoned Neglected

Depressed Agitated Alone Fearful Vulnerable

Hopeless Weak Angry Worthless Powerless Broken

Tormented Rejected Insignificant Frightened Overwhelmed

Overlooked Hopeless Unloved Used

Awkward Confused Hurt In despair Aggrieved

Ruined Odd

PART TWO – THE AFTERMATH

(DIARY ENTRY – MAY 14ᵀᴴ 2000)

Today in my heart I feel angry and betrayed. I feel beaten, like I am on a roundabout that won't stop. How do I see the glory? When all I do at times is destroy myself? You see there is this void in me that I keep filling with things to run away from my despair. Drinking, cutting myself, having unwanted sex, when all I need is a cuddle. Truthfully all I need is to love myself. How do you love yourself? I've tried fixing myself up; hair, clothes, make up but when I open my mouth anger comes out. But my heart is longing to be free, to fly like a bird to let it all out, to the sky. Rage, hurt, anger be FREE.

Somebody calm my bruised heart, soothe my spirit. Hold on heart, hold onto me, hold on so I can find myself. I am willing to try to get support and encouragement. Hold on.

HOW SEXUAL ABUSE AFFECTED MY LIFE

Whilst in care (13–17 years old) I managed to avoid engaging in a productive way with the therapeutic services that were made available to me to address how past sexual abuse was affecting my life. I had every opportunity to get support but I could not fully commit myself to the process and tried my best to avoid engaging with key workers assigned to help me. Instead, I spent most of my time participating in destructive behaviour that was not conducive to my well-being. At 14 years old I started drinking alcohol, closely followed by smoking cigarettes and weed. Getting high was an outlet to forget the sadness and confusion that had become my everyday reality. I started to self-harm and my self-esteem was so poor I believed I was nothing but trash. I dabbled with sniffing solvents whilst in Middlesex Lodge, a secure home for girls that I was sent to for unmanageable behaviour. All the other girls did it and used it as a substitute when they could not get weed or alcohol. I tried it once but did not like the taste so I stuck with cigarettes when I could not get my substance of choice. Most of the friends I had in care, girls and boys, had been sexually abused, neglected and physically abused; we all dealt with our pain in different ways. I suffered nightmares and was full of fear because of what happened to me, but on the outside, in some of the kid's homes I was sent to I was trying to make others fear me because I believed being in control would make me feel secure. It was a constant cycle of negative behaviour that I actively embraced and participated in. It was after I found myself pregnant at 16 years old, unable to run and hide from constant memories, nightmares and emotions, that the slow realisation of how sexual abuse affected my life started to hit home and affected me in the following ways:

- **Post-traumatic stress disorder**: diagnosed at 13 years old. Post-traumatic stress disorder is an anxiety disorder caused by stressful, frightening or distressing events. I had nightmares, anxiety, difficulty concentrating, difficulty sleeping and irritability. This condition was persistent in my life for many years.
- **Mental health issues**: two nervous breakdowns as a result of a build-up of issues, anxiety problems, depression, phobia of crowded places.
- **Suicidal thoughts and attempts**: when I could not express how I was feeling, thoughts of suicide led to overdosing on paracetamol. More often cries for help than actual serious attempts to kill myself.
- **Anger problems**: hitting other people, breaking things, being verbally abusive – especially in care to those in authority
- **Self-harm**: could not articulate inner emotional pain. Cutting arms and legs with razors felt like a good outlet to vent anger and the helplessness I felt inside.
- **Sleep problems**: found it hard to get to sleep; once asleep had reoccurring nightmares from abuse. Would get to sleep late at night and wake up unusually early, and then sleep in the day.
- **Flashbacks**: random thoughts would be triggered by certain smells, music, and food from my childhood.
- **Promiscuity/Sexualised behaviour**: I am not proud to admit this, but because of the abuse, I would let boys touch me sexually. Earliest I can remember was at around 14 years old. I never had sex until I was 16 years old as I always stopped before it got to that point. But once I did have sex, it became an issue because it then became something I could not control. No value

of self and weak boundaries led me into inappropriate, short-lived relationships; I felt unable to say no past a certain point because I believed I had led them on.

• **Poor self-esteem and confidence**: did not like myself and felt unworthy of anything good or positive in life. I found it hard to believe I could achieve my goals and dreams or that I could turn my life around.

• **Compulsive and obsessive behaviours**: shopping, hoarding or obsessive thoughts about material things until I acquired them; excessive spending on things I did not need. Double checking doors, windows, even going all the way somewhere to go all the way back to double check. Also unhealthy need to be in control of circumstances that I could not possibly control!

• **Poor relationship choices**: fuelled by low self-esteem and witnessing my parents' own abusive relationship model, the first relationship I ended up in was emotionally and physically abusive. I had trust issues and kept men at an emotional distance.

• **Secretiveness**: I did not reveal much about myself to anyone and I ensured that continued by isolating myself. I was scared of being rejected or judged.

• **Substance abuse** (weed and alcohol): many will argue smoking weed/marijuana in itself is not abusive or addictive; however it became addictive for me as I used it as a form of escapism between the ages of 14 and 21 years old to escape my reality, insecurities and memories of the abuse.

Besides the emotional, psychological and behavioural effects past abuse had on my life, I had to cope with and adapt from the age of 13 years old to having no family support. My family were all I had known until that point but when I spoke out and was taken into care, everything changed. It was a struggle to adjust and if I am honest, it took me many years even after leaving care to settle down into life. I had little contact with my brother and sister. My siblings were divided in what they believed. My brother remembered me being sneaked out of the house and backed me that I was telling the truth, whilst my sister did the same at one point but changed her mind in order to remain part of the family. My brother and sister were placed on a child protection register after I was taken into care. The fallout from my disclosure was great in the aftermath, and I do not have a relationship with any of my birth family to this day. Apart from what I have shared about how sexual abuse affected my life, there are other issues that can affect the survivor.

HOW SEXUAL ABUSE CAN AFFECT PEOPLE IN THE AFTERMATH – EMOTIONAL, PSYCHOLOGICAL, BEHAVIOURAL

- Depression;
- Eating disorders (anorexia, bulimia);
- Drug addictions/substance misuse issues (drug, alcohol);
- Risky behaviours (promiscuity);
- Anxiety disorders;
- Personality disorders;
- Intimacy and relationship problems;
- Phobias;
- Hyperactivity;
- Excessive behaviours;
- Sleep disorders (nightmares, trouble falling asleep/staying awake);
- Self-harm (cutting, pulling out hair);
- Suicide attempts;
- Dysfunctional relationships;
- Isolation – lack of involvement with people or outside world;
- Sexual dysfunction.

The impact of sexual abuse can be different for each person. The impact it can have on emotional, mental health, relationship and life choices should not be taken lightly. It does not matter if you were sexually abused once or repeatedly – you must never minimalise the impact of your experience as less important than anyone else, because in doing so is to undermine the severity of the impact it has had on your life. It is a known fact that many survivors do not tell anyone what happened to them or if they do, they do not disclose the abuse until years later.

Experts in the field of interfamilial and childhood sexual abuse have stated in research findings that a number of determining factors lead to a better outcome for the survivor in healing from the traumatic impact of their abuse, such as family support, relationship to the abuser, how long the abuse lasted, intrusiveness of the abuse, how soon disclosure was made and whether the sexual abuse was penetrative or not.

By carrying the burden of such a devastating secret from childhood into adulthood, it can manifest itself in many different ways in the survivor's life. If you have tried to ignore and forget what has happened to you, it is important that you get support to acknowledge first to yourself that you were sexually abused. It is the biggest and hardest step of your journey to healing. It takes courage to admit what has happened to you, but in order to start the process of healing, this step – which is key to reclaiming your life – cannot be avoided.

◆ EMPOWER POINT – ACKNOWLEDGING MY PAST

Write down one thing you would be willing to try to help you address what has happened to you. In this space provided, try to answer the questions the best way you can. It does not have to be done in one sitting – you may come back when you want and answer them in your own time. As mentioned, self-acknowledgement is the first major step in your journey.

• What has been your experience? (Share as little or as much as you like.)

• How has past sexual abuse affected your life?

• Is there anything on the lists I mentioned that you identify as having had issues with?

• Is there anything on your list you would like to address and get help for?

• Is there anything on that list that you have overcome? How does that make you feel?

(DIARY ENTRY - MAY 2002)

WHAT I LOST

Sexual abuse has taken a lot away from me. I am now in my twenties and I have just realised this. I'm in therapy again and this time it is really raw. I know everything – my secretiveness, attitude towards myself, sexual behaviour – all stem from my past experience. One of the main things that has been destroyed for me is ME. All the things as a child I was supposed to have (innocence, love) were taken from me, so it has really been a guessing game of who I am supposed to be. Ever since then I have tried to be what everyone else expects me to be. I do want to be able to accept me because when I have those foundations in myself I will be part way to loving me, so when people say things about me I won't fall to pieces. I don't think I really have allowed myself to grieve about everything that has happened to me. I don't know, I have suffered with depression for 13 years and been clinically depressed for the last two, so I don't know if depression is classed as grieving. I have never sat down and really cried about my father. I did love him but I don't now. As for my mother, all I have ever felt towards her is anger and frustration, now I am not even angry at her anymore, as a matter of fact I don't even think about her. I think I am repressing these feelings and have detached myself from it all. The only pain I feel is about me. I am very frustrated at myself, frustrated at being needy, frustrated at wanting other people's approval all the time and not respecting myself.

MY BATTLE WITH MAJOR ISSUES

I want to share with you in more detail some of the major personal challenges I have battled with to various degrees in the aftermath of abuse. I found these issues extremely difficult to cope with at times and in the midst of the darkness of my journey, these issues left me disheartened and discouraged, wondering if I would ever live a life free from the traumatic effect of my childhood. I have gained victory in some issues, but in others, the struggle is being battled on a daily basis. In the midst of all the complexity within my emotions, relational breakdowns and mental health issues, I have had to learn to grieve for the loss of so much. In the chapter titled 'Support', I will share with you some exercises that have helped in the midst of the journey to healing.

Depression

When I was 10 years old, a year into my sexual abuse, a sense of darkness and sadness came upon me that mentally stayed with me from that point on for many years. That darkness was medically diagnosed as depression when I was 13 years old. Over the next twenty years, depression made my life unbearable when caught in its debilitating grip. Contrary to what some people may think, depression is not being miserable or unhappy, it affects the very core of a person's soul, and left undiagnosed and untreated can cause serious problems. As you can see from my poem titled 'Burden', at my lowest point depression affected my ability to do even the smallest of tasks. Like an uninvited guest, depression would turn up unexpectedly and stay for varied times ranging from weeks to months. I would forget to eat or not have an appetite, found it hard to concentrate, cry all the time. I isolated myself from the outside world as I found it hard to be around people, which meant lengthy absences from work. I had no hope in anything, and thoughts of ending it all consumed my mind often.

I spent many days in bed feeling sad and tearful because I struggled with what happened to me as a child. I grew frustrated with myself because I had not 'got over it' yet. In the darkness of my depression, I tried several half-hearted suicide attempts that were more a cry for help than actually wanting to die; I wanted to be free of the pain I felt inside – I literally felt I was dying in pain. I could not articulate the overwhelming feelings I was battling with daily and wanted the despair to end. I was broken in heart and in spirit. (*The human spirit can endure in sickness, but a crushed spirit who can bear? – Proverbs 18:14*)

I would go to bed late and wake up several times in the night, which only added to my inability to function during the day; depression affected my sleeping pattern. Depression was like having a clamp squeezing my brain, it constricted my every movement and thought. When I had my first nervous breakdown at 22 years old, that was when everything in my life came crashing down. I was such a wreck that I was put on three different types of medication to help me function. I was put on medication because of the severity of depression and the anxiety attacks that were not helped by nightmares and lack of sleep. Initially, the medication helped for a while and I was on them for two years, but the side effects of taking such medication were horrible. I sweated profusely, got tremors and shakes whilst sleeping and at random moments throughout the day, and I felt like a zombie as my bodily movements operated in delayed motion. When I was discharged from the hospital, I started psychotherapy.

Over the two years I met with the psychotherapist, I began to open up about how my dad sexually abused me. This was my first real attempt at facing my past without creating distractions to not deal with the deep-rooted issues left behind, and it was extremely painful. The process left me feeling vulnerable at times. I began to see how the abuse affected my life and realised I had not grieved for my loss. I didn't realise I was allowed to grieve my past – for what happened to me; I was always made to feel that I should have been over it a long time ago and that I was being negative in talking about it. The pain that I felt did not matter to the people I had in my life back then, but when I look back I can see I was seeking validation and approval from people that had no real interest in me being emotionally well. I allowed myself to feel the full emotion of my feelings. I grieved for the loss of my innocence, loss of family relationships, my childhood, injustice, betrayal, disappointment in my mum and dad, loss of years spent trying to cope in the aftermath, and the many other things that I have had to count as a loss. Coming to terms with my loss, understanding the abuse was not my fault and learning to find my true identity were all key parts of helping me find release from depression.

Forgiveness

Having the time and space each week for someone to listen to me without judgement, no matter how crazy some of my statements sounded made a huge impact on my journey to healing. Up until the point I started therapy, I had a deep hatred for my dad. The anger I felt towards him was intense and I did not wish him well. In not getting justice for the suffering caused to me and him not being held accountable for the damage he inflicted, I condemned and punished myself with my self-destructive behaviour. I had to learn to forgive; not as an act to let him off the hook but to release myself from the grip hatred had on my heart and life. I learned over time to forgive those who caused me emotional turmoil. I had to forgive, not only to be released from the poison of its bondage but because Christ forgave me when I did not deserve it. It may seem crazy that I would forgive my parents for their treatment of me but the inner release of peace that I have had since has lifted a huge burden from my shoulders. I cannot logically explain it; it is something that comes from a personal encounter with Jesus being reborn in the spirit. *(The person without the Spirit (spirit of Christ Jesus) does not accept the things that come from the Spirit of God but considers them foolishness, and cannot understand them because they are discerned only through the Spirit – 1 Corinthians 2:14)*

God is kind and gracious to all of us whether Christian or non-Christian, but it is through Jesus we can get help in the midst of the darkness of depression of the soul. *(Come to me, all you who are weary and burdened and I will give you rest – Matthew 11:28)*

When I was 21 years old, in the presence of my mum and brother, I confronted my dad about what he had done to me as a child. He called me a liar and was dismissive and angry at me turning up at their house. My motivation for going was my mum always said, if he did this to me why had I not confronted him, so I did but I left that house enraged, upset and no further down the road to closure or vindication. The cycle of depression, hatred and anger continued to suffocate my life and it felt like it would never end. It was on reading an article, years ago that I reflected on that encounter with my dad and it made me realise I was at a crossroads in how I allowed him and my past abuse to further affect my life. It read:

'Someone has caused you great pain, despair, misery. You confront them fist raging, ranting about the impact their actions had on your life, and when you finish venting you expect an apology, recognition of some kind for the offence they caused but instead they turn to you and say, "That is your problem, not mine" – what do you do then?'

I knew at that point I had a decision to make and through gritted teeth I chose to forgive him. It was not easy and the process took years to do. You may not be at a point of asking yourself the question, 'Am I going to allow the perpetrator and my past experience of sexual abuse to have an effect on my life and future?' and that is okay. Your priority may be to just cope with every day or deal with the tears, anger and pain you have suffered – that is understandable. My question to you is, has it bred contempt and hatred in your soul towards the abuser? If so that is understandable too but hatred is like a poison you are left to drink that will corrode your soul and leave you bitter. This could not possibly be what you really want for yourself?

Whilst you carry the guilt, blame and shame of being abused and the burden of the perpetrator's poor choices, the perpetrator continues to live their life unperturbed, possibly not giving a second thought to the damage their destructiveness has caused you.

Regardless of whether I ever get my day of justice in the courts of this land, I had to make a choice. The choice was to choose to continue to be a prisoner of my past – waiting for acknowledgement from people who do not care or who cannot admit they're wrong – or I could choose to take whatever positive steps, however hard, to rebuild my life. It does not mean I forget nor does it mean I want a relationship with my birth dad but I also have the gift of free will so I made the choice to release myself from the burden of the consequences of my parents' actions.

The issue of forgiveness is something over the years I have to keep bringing back to God and praying about because when those times of anger, pain and personal difficulty come to remind me of where it came from, it causes me to remember who committed the offence against me. I cannot forgive in my own strength so I ask Jesus to help me and he does. I need help not just to forgive others but also to forgive me for how I coped in the midst of my trauma, and the harm some of my choices did to me.

Support and understanding proved to be pivotal in helping me move on towards building a new foundation for my life. It took time to build trust with my therapist, but it was a relationship built on good communication and understanding. Whilst she did listen to me express myself she also provided advice, knowledge and gave me the mental tools to help me learn a new way of dealing not only with my depression but also with my emotions and everyday life. I became a born-again Christian at the lowest point in my life just before I was admitted to the hospital for having a nervous breakdown. Having a relationship with Jesus was not a magic formula, but it gave me hope, peace and release from the burden of my problems. I still had to work through all my challenges; it is a work that continues to this day.

From the age of 22 to 37 years old, the severity of my depression deepened before but it started to lessen over time. I have indeed been freed from the clutches of depression and the last time I had a serious episode was five years ago. I still get periods of low moods and anxiety from time to time, but Jesus is healing and restoring me. (*He who the son sets free is free indeed – John 8:36*)

Rejection

Being rejected in any situation is bad enough but when you are rejected as a child for something that is not your fault that has been committed against you; then ostracised for speaking out, it is truly devastating. I was rejected because I refused to live a lie and I suffered handsomely for it. My mum knew the truth but chose to stick by my dad and reject me. At 21 years old, I made the decision not to continue a relationship with her anymore as her denial, avoidance of conversations surrounding my abuse and lack of empathy were too much. Out of all my family, only my brother stood by me and the sad thing is because of the way the revelation of abuse broke the family and the subsequent things that happened in the aftermath, our relationship has also broken down. The foundations of my birth family were built on lies and secrets so it is not surprising that when my abuse came to light, the foundation easily broke down, but that is not my fault.

I was used to emotional rejection by my mum from a young age but as I grew older it became harder to ignore. I found myself trying to hold on to a non-existent emotional relationship with her in exchange for having her presence in my life. In the end, it caused me more harm than good and deeply contributed to the depression I was experiencing. One memory forever sticks in my mind in relation to her rejection of me and that was the day I saw her on a train when I was coming from work. I was at one end of the carriage and she was at the other and I knew she saw me as I definitely saw her. She pretended not to see me and walked right down the carriage into another one. I remember I just sat in my seat, hot tears brimming in my eyes. I do not know what I was expecting as it had been years

70

since our relationship ceased; maybe some type of acknowledgement of my existence. But that day as I got home and curled up crying in my bed, I understood that this was my cost for standing in truth and it was devastating.

If you have faced a similar situation, I want to let you know you are not alone. There is no easy way to face the brutality of rejection and I know it sounds cliché but time does prove to be a healer in such circumstances. The pain of the experience may seem like it will never go away but it does lessen over time. You will have to ride through the waves of emotions that come with rejection; loss and heartbreak that at times feel extremely raw. It is okay to cry about the unfairness of it all. I cried a lot for many years about the rejection of my mum, but one day sometime later, the memory of her snub did not hurt anymore and it was then I realised I had come to terms with the situation.

Life is a cycle and there is a process that happens in many things relating to it. I cried, I mourned, I moved on. This was the process I had to go through in order to let go. As I was in therapy during this time, it helped me to not to take her rejection personally. God also showed me that he would be the parent I never had. (*A father to the fatherless, a defender of widows, is God in his holy dwelling – Psalm 65:5-6*). I gained something greater.

Parenting

I have found being a mother and parenting difficult at times, even though I love and care for my daughters the same, the circumstances have been different. Back twenty years ago as a single parent at 17 years old, I had ongoing mental health issues, was in an emotionally and physically abusive relationship with an ex-boyfriend and trying to cope with issues left behind because of sexual abuse. I looked after my first-born daughter's emotional well-being; provided hugs, kisses, speaking words of encouragement, showing love to her, but my capacity to function fully was affected by periods of crippling depression and low self-esteem. Whilst trying to be her mother I was also struggling to come to terms with the rejection of my own mum. I was a young girl lost, not yet at a point of dealing with the pain of my own experiences, and not having a tangible example of how to love and nurture my own daughter meant I learned to parent on the run. Being thrown straight in the deep end of life, from the instability of the care system into the demands of motherhood, was stressful. Emotionally I struggled to swim against the waves of sudden change, but the reality was I had to adapt very fast – and I just about managed. I had to live a life of a grown woman from a young age, and for a time circumstances dictated the path my life was taking. I never had time to think about my decisions but I never regretted having my children.

I noticed when my first daughter turned 9 years old, I became emotionally stuck. Every decision I made I second guessed and was full of self-doubt as I wondered if I was the best person to mother my child. I remember feeling overwhelmed and scared about not being able to provide her with the continued love and stability that she deserved and needed, and I was scared I could not protect her from sexual abuse. I could not find a point of reference for me to relate to her at this particular age and that made me panic inside. I could see the parallels between how I was withdrawing from my child to when I was first sexually abused at 9 years old and needed my mum the most.

Dealing with insecurities and fears that can surface during parenting as a survivor can bring up feelings of vulnerability that can be overwhelming even with support. The issue has never been about any of my daughters, rather it has been about my ability to believe that I could love them past the age where my own pain started. What I have learned is just because I was birthed from my mum does not mean I inherited her style of parenting or that I will make the same choices that she did. I am slowly learning not to be hard on myself about my shortcomings as a parent and circumstances outside of my control. I am not the perfect parent but I choose to focus on my strengths and get support in the areas I struggle with. What I learned from my first parenting experience, I am using to help parent my second daughter. I was able to work with a psychotherapist through these emotions and that helped me to understand why those fears existed and helped me to manage and look beyond them. I offer myself to my daughters emotionally, and I am confident through the love Jesus has given to me I can use this to build meaningful relationships with both of my daughters.

Anger

As a teenager in care, I expressed my anger outwardly by smashing things and indulging in destructive behaviour. I naively thought because my plate smashing days were long behind me that my anger issues had magically resolved, but the truth is it began to manifest itself in other areas of my life. I was confrontational and defensive over the most trivial of situations and would get upset very quickly. I knew something was wrong with my irrational behaviour over the years but could not figure out what it was. Sometimes if I had an argument with my husband, which happens between couples from time to time, I would literally feel myself shaking with rage. It would rise up out of nowhere and I would lose my temper and get angry at myself, later regretting not handling the situation better. I would also get angry if I did not do things right the first time and if I made mistakes I never gave myself a break. It was only through prayer and years of therapy I realised the root of my anger stemmed from the injustice of my situation, the helplessness I felt about myself and the powerlessness I felt as a child. I was angry at my inability to heal quicker on my own timescale, and the fact these were issues was still hindering my life.

Even though I didn't think about my past abuse every day, subconsciously my mind still held it as an unresolved issue in need of closure. As I did not make the connection that I was still hurt about my past, I turned the anger inwards and punished myself, struggling with self-harming from the age of 14 years old until the age of 30. One clear sign of progress in dealing with anger issues is that I haven't self-harmed for the last decade. It has been hard to accept that I have received no justice but I am learning to trust that God will deliver justice in my situation; I have to trust he will repay for the wrongs done to me. I am learning to be kind to myself by focusing on the positive progress I have made and, in the past, have written a letter to the person who abused me as an exercise in venting some of my frustrations.

I have discovered other issues that I did not connect with the abuse and just put down to my character and personality. For instance, I never connected my need for control stemmed out of the helplessness I felt as a child. I slowly started to recognise this in my marriage when it came to decision-making discussions with my husband. I would take his need for clarification or trying to get me to agree to things that would be beneficial to both of us and our family as him trying to control me. I wanted things to go my way without compromise and if I felt threatened by any conversation, I would become completely rigid, only able to see things in black and white. Because I became aware of this connection, I went back to counselling to get the help I need and now am learning to have a much more balanced relationship with my husband. It is okay to feel anger as long as you recognise it for what it is and seek help to identify the root cause so that it does not become destructive. Healthy avenues involve taking a step back from the situation, talking and writing things down instead of angry outbursts, emotional self-harm or denial.

I have accepted on my journey to self-discovery and healing from abuse that my experience has affected me in many ways but God in his love and kindness has kept me this far and is slowly healing and restoring me. It was never God's will that I suffer abuse nor was it his will for you to suffer either. An example of his kindness towards me is that he did not reveal or allow the weight of memories of my abuse to bombard me all at once – otherwise, I would have been overwhelmed and crushed under the hopelessness of it. The trauma of sexual abuse is so painful and intrusive that it has the ability to leave you feeling totally helpless and vulnerable, and that can place you in situations that are not good for your well-being. Everything happened at the time it was supposed to. (*Everything happens at the appointed time –Ecclesiastes 3:1*) The gradual unveiling of painful memories and information from my past life helped me process it in a way that would not lead to further destruction. This is why support is important in taking those steps in facing what has happened to you.

THE MASK

This is the day I can clearly pinpoint developing 'the mask'. Back in the eighties, the Kodak camera was the must-have item gadget wise. The Kodak camera was a cool and fun way to capture life's precious moments because photos printed in an instant. I hated having my picture taken because I always felt uncomfortable. My dad took most of the family photos, and Christmas time was no different. I was 10 years old in this photo and I clearly remember every minute leading up to this picture being taken. Just five minutes earlier, I was lying on my bed crying about what was happening in my life and I distinctly remembered feeling trapped and alone. I remember quietly slipping away from my family downstairs in the living room and going upstairs to the privacy of the bedroom that I shared with my sister. Behind the closed door, tears flowed down my face and the pain I felt emotionally and physically caused me to curl into the tiniest of human balls. For those precious few minutes, I could stop pretending to be the happy, vibrant little girl called Yvonne and just be the confused and frightened girl who was dying inside with a secret I had no name for.

If sexual abuse were packaged with a survival kit for victims and survivors, the mask would be the 'must-have' item to have. The mask took up residence in my life soon after the sexual abuse began and I learned to use it as a front to hide my sadness, guilt and shame from the outside world. I had done nothing wrong, I had nothing to hide but I felt in some way to blame for what was happening to me. The mask allowed me to be secretive about my emotions, to pretend all was okay. In private I would be sad; in public, I laughed and joked around, pretending not to have a care in the world with a fake smile spread across my face. No one saw under the mask, the fear when wash time came or the tears I cried and hid in my face flannel after my dad indecently assaulted me night after night in the bathroom. I had no control over what happened to my body or me, but what I could control was how I appeared to the outside world. Not only my protector, over time my mask also became my deceiver because behind closed doors it isolated me from connecting with me as I self-harmed and indulged in other self-destructive behaviours.

Wearing a mask of normalcy while living in a state of emotional alertness became more tiring to live with the older I got. I did try to take off the mask a few times – well if I am being honest, it began to slip off. Therapy helped me to open up and identify why I hid behind the mask for over twenty years, and provided a safe environment for me to take it off. What helped me to keep operating behind the mask was the belief that I thought I was good at hiding my emotions, but as much as I thought I hid my despair well, people from different eras of my past commented there was always a sense of sadness about me. I thought the mask was hiding my true emotions but people saw through the façade.

Having the right environment and taking my time to explore these feelings helped me to see with clarity that the shame, guilt and condemnation I carried since a child and hid behind the mask for fear of judgement, was never mine to carry. Through connecting with other survivors, I realised that I was not the only survivor who wore a mask to hide the shame of a crime that corroded my self-esteem and worth as a human being. I gained bravery through strength in God to step out from behind the mask and face me.

Maybe you are reading this as someone who recognises the mask too well. In front of your family, friends, people you work with or when dealing with people in the outside world, you feel unable to let anyone see you vulnerable or see you as you truly are. It is a natural reaction after all you have been through to protect yourself. With the wrong people you should always be cautious but with the right people who have your best interests at heart, who can support you, you can slowly reveal the person behind the mask.

There is nothing worse than feeling transparent and vulnerable – as we were as children – and have it used as a weapon against you. As victims in our childhood and survivors of our past, I can fully empathise and understand your concerns. I want to encourage you as someone who has finally taken off the mask and shown the world through my openness in sharing my personal experiences, it is liberating not having to hide or pretend anymore. I took courage from daring to hope that I could heal and be free to be my own person. It is a slow process of learning how to face difficult feelings and fears, placing the blame where it belongs (on the perpetrator of your abuse) and having the courage to take one step at a time to discover who you really are. One thing I know for certain; the mask only helps to a certain point but in the end, you will have to face what is behind the mask. You.

◆ EMPOWER POINT – THE MASK

Do you recognise the mask?

On the mask below write how you present yourself to the outside world. So, for instance you could write on it happy, confident etc.

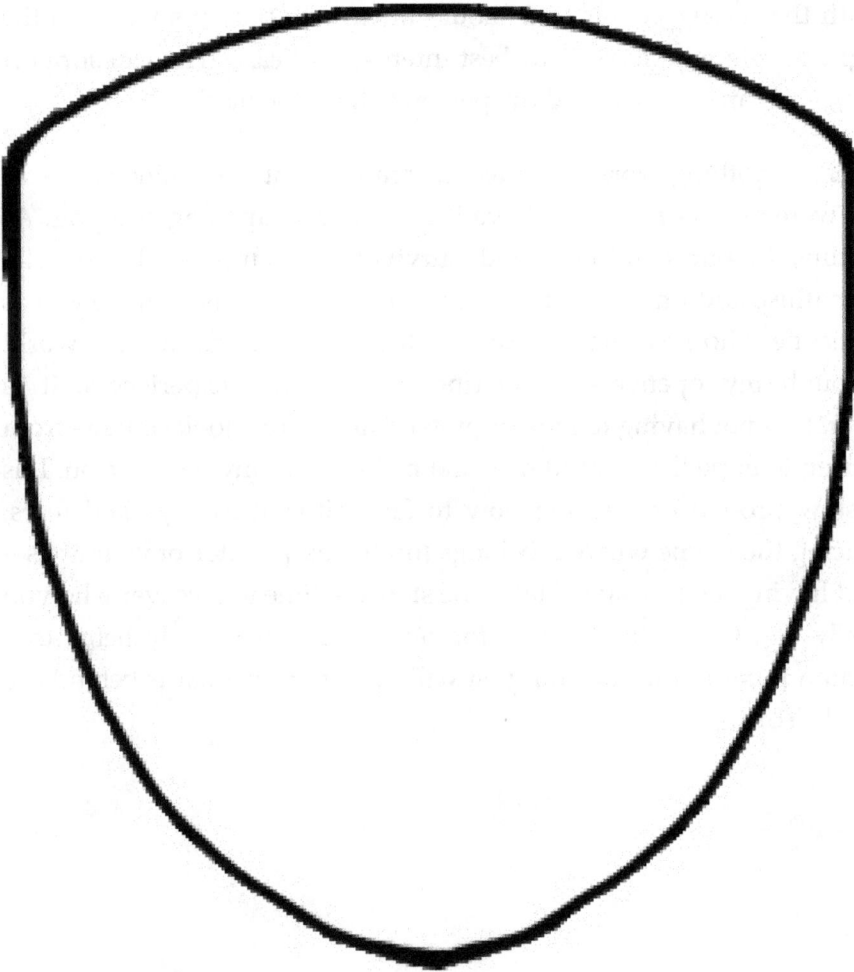

• What age were you when you first recognised 'the mask'?

• How does your mask help you to hide your feelings?

- Do you fear showing people the real you? Why?

• What would encourage you to face what is underneath your mask?

◆ EMPOWER POINT

Explore one of the options you wrote down that would encourage
you to face the feelings and fears hidden beneath your mask. Imagine
you had the perfect way to do it. How would you go about it?

BURDEN

(Poem I wrote in 1999)

Someone carry these bags for me, that are on my back

My mind is as sharp as it has always been

But my spirit and body are weak and tired

Tears I have cried so long

Under my duvet the hours and days have gone

I give simple instructions to my mind –

Breathe in Yvonne, breathe out

Stand up straight Yvonne

People will know something is wrong if you slouch

So many thoughts run through my mind

If God is the ultimate judge

My Father's punishment, when will it be and what kind?

And I am a Mother who loves her child

So how could my Mother be with him an abuser so vile?

See my mind is still there to think of such circumstances as such

I am hurt still

But you say forgiveness is a must

Jesus is my hero

Because he carried that cross on his back ridiculed by his foes

But he suffered for you and me

So until my day of glory comes

I will struggle by with these bags

That hurt my being

But for me at this edge

Seeing really is believing

I wasted my faith and hope

And just like my cigarettes

Frustration, despair, anticipation –

my spirit feels like it has all gone up in smoke

No one prepared me for being a child

No one warned me of sexual abuse so vile

Weakness fills my veins

I have the sanity to write this so I'm not insane

Breathe in Yvonne, breathe out

Because in all this thinking

One day you will be victorious

To sing and shout

Yvonne

PART THREE – FACING THE PAST

(DIARY ENTRY – MAY 25TH 2000)

I feel like giving up on myself, even though I know I have not started to work on me. Time. Time is what I have on my side but patience is something I never had. All I know is that I feel lonely. Night after night and drink after drink, alcohol has become my best friend. When the loneliness kicks in I drink a bottle or two. I know the decisions I need to make and deep down the answer cannot be found in a bottle of wine or a man. What do I do now? Only God knows.

SPEAKING OUT – SOME TRUTHS I NEED TO SHARE WITH YOU

If you are considering speaking out, I feel it is important to share with you some truths I have discovered in coming out from behind the secrecy of sexual abuse on my journey to healing and recovery. Acknowledging your abuse will not be easy. It requires strength, support and courage to see the process through and it can take a long time. I learned first-hand that using distractions to avoid dealing with the past only delays the inevitable. The memories do not just go away, and in order to heal from the trauma you must face what has happened to you in its entirety, otherwise directly or indirectly it will continue to have an effect on your life.

The biggest hurdle you will have to first overcome is acknowledging to yourself what has happened to you. I sometimes take for granted how hard that is because of how far I have come on my own journey. Why is it hard to do? I believe it stems from fear of what lies on the other side of acknowledgement and disclosure. That fear is not easy to describe because it has felt ever present. It lived with me as part of my new reality inherited along with the experience of sexual abuse.

Maybe you fear to face the truth of what has happened to you; the memories, betrayal, guilt, shame or the devastation and loss sexual abuse has left behind. It may appear that to acknowledge your abuse will be just as painful as the violation of being abused; it is very painful, I cannot deny that. But in time the pain lessens as you face each part of all that your abuse has taken from you.

Facing your past may lead you to try and understand and seek answers to questions you may never get answers to, and that can be disappointing and even make you feel hopeless for a while; but the key focus of recovery, which will come with time, is reclaiming your life. The process of healing will take you to a deep unknown place within you, and to reclaim your life, you must go through it. It is a journey over time that will release you from the bondage abuse has you bound in, and what you will eventually gain is the freedom to view your life and make choices from a different standpoint to live the life you choose.

You may ask yourself the question 'How can I start to address what has happened to me if I am not sure what happened to me is sexual abuse or how it has affected me?'

I think in order to find the answers, you will need to explore these questions with a counselling professional. Whether it happened once, twice or repeated times, a violation of this kind is bound to have an effect. Minimising the abuse, avoidance and using distractions are some of the coping mechanisms used by survivors to cope with their abuse. This is a normal occurrence for many survivors trying to live with the dysfunction and abnormality of living with trauma. Survivors have in their own way developed coping methods to deal with everyday life, but the truth is these methods only help for a certain amount of time before the issue comes to a head.

When I was 19 years old, I was a broken and lost young woman. No words could articulate the pain and craziness I felt inside and there was no one around me that I could relate to. One day someone gave me a book by an author called Joyce Meyer, titled 'Tell them I love them', and for the first time in my life, I found someone that could articulate what I was going through. This middle-aged white evangelist woman who lived on the other side of the world who, if put side by side with me you would never think we would have anything in common, gave voice to my inner struggles through her gift of writing, and I am grateful that book came my way; it was like finding treasure in a dark place.

I wish during my teens someone had openly shared his or her story with me the way I am openly sharing with you. During my teenage years, whilst I was in care, many of my peers – girls and boys – had been abused but no one ever talked about it; you only saw the pain and destruction left, by the way we all lashed out. I wish someone had been brave enough to tell me the truth about some of the challenges and realisations that I would face on speaking out and how difficult the journey would be to healing. I may not have at the time been able to fully comprehend the value of this precious advice and knowledge, but at least the seeds of its importance would have been sown in my soul for a time when I could reap their meaning. This is why I am sharing my experience with you. For when the lies of your past try to creep into your mind in moments of vulnerability, remember the truths I am about to share with you. This is just a phase in your journey. You can and will make it through.

YOU ARE NOT TO BLAME

One of the major issues that I have found many survivors of sexual abuse struggle with is guilt and shame. For many years I felt that because I was a lively, playful child, this was the cause of my abuse; that because of my personality, I attracted this horrible attention. I have come to learn and understand over the years that even if I cartwheeled around the house in my underwear; even if I walked around naked, I still would not be to blame. A child can never be responsible for the actions of an adult because the power, control, authority and influence are disproportionate. My dad, the adult in our relationship, is solely responsible for his actions. He chose with his own free will to abuse me; I am not responsible for his actions, and neither are you responsible for the perpetrator of your abuse. No matter who the abuser is – sibling, family friend or acquaintance, cousin, babysitter – they had no right to abuse you. You are not to blame in any way, shape or form for their actions. No one has the right to violate you in any way, EVEN if your body reacted in a way a body does to the stimulus, it still does not make you at fault.

As uncomfortable as it is to acknowledge, the fact is the body does react to stimulus. I believe it is important for us to address this as it has caused many survivors to feel damned. I felt damned for many years because of this, and it caused me to not fully disclose my abuse; the shame of it hindered my healing. I never enjoyed what he was doing but my body reacted to being stimulated in this way. This further added to my belief that I deserved what happened to me. I thought I was bad; what other explanation could there be for why my dad would do this to me? Coupled together with the physical reactions of my body deceiving me into thinking I enjoyed it, I felt like I had done something to feel guilty about.

In my autobiography, 'Daughter Arise', I talk about the struggle I had with the guilt and shame of what happened to me. It was in psychotherapy in my early twenties that I began to understand the truth about sexual abuse and accept I was not to blame. It took time but the realisation dawned on me when faced with truth and facts. This is where an unshakeable foundation of truth is needed to stand on because feelings and emotions will deceive you into thinking you caused your own abuse. This foundation has to be something outside the manipulation of your own thoughts, emotions and feelings. I found that foundation in Christ Jesus who has set me free from condemnation. *(There is now no condemnation in Christ Jesus – Romans 8:1)* You are not to blame so please do not condemn yourself. You cannot carry the burden of other people's actions. It does not matter what the perpetrator, family or friends believe or say. The fact is, the guilt and shame are not yours to carry, and releasing yourself from this lie will be life-changing and important.

SILENCE IS NOT GOLDEN

Sexual abuse is such a complex and overwhelming issue that it is no wonder many victims and survivors choose not to tell anybody. While it can seem a better option not to speak out, in the long run, it can cause more harm than good.

It is difficult to know what to do because of the different dilemmas that you have to consider. You may love the perpetrator but hate what they have done to you and feel conflicted because you don't want them to get in trouble, or you may be scared of what people, especially loved ones may think of you. These dilemmas may lead you to a decision not to disclose your abuse, but it is important for you to know that child abusers and paedophiles, people who commit these crimes, are more than likely to have done it before or since – they do not deserve your protection. (*The 1994 National health survey (US) of 453 paedophiles conducted by Dr. Gene Abel showed these criminals were collectively responsible for the molestation of 67,000 children – 148 per paedophile.*) These individuals are a danger to society; they are opportunists who wait for a situation to manipulate, groom and abuse a vulnerable child. They inoculate and isolate their victim to make them believe they are the only one they have abused, which makes them feel it is their fault.

The truth is there are no guarantees of the outcome if you make a decision to speak out, but what I do know is your decision definitely has to be about you. This has to be your foundation as I have seen survivors left broken by the law process when the police or Crown Prosecution Service do not take their case any further, or when the courts do not sentence the perpetrator or give them a sentence less than what they believe is deserved.

Speaking out was a two-tier process for me: my initial disclosure to a friend at 13 years old; then at 22 years old, talking through my actual abuse with a professional counsellor. The best analogy I can use to describe my avoidance up to this point is that of a rubbish bin. The bin (me) was full of rubbish (destructive behaviours, avoidance of dealing with issues, etc.) that instead of being emptied out (dealing with issues by talking) kept being filled with more rubbish, whilst trying to force down the lid (function and cope with everyday life)! I kept putting off dealing with the root of my problems, and every time I attempted to lift the lid of the bin (face pain by dealing with the issues) the rubbish (destructiveness behaviours) would spill out! It was because I could no longer close the bin lid that led to my first nervous breakdown in my early twenties. The pressure and stress of keeping something so traumatising inside can cause long-term mental and psychological problems. It took me nine years to get to that point, and thirty years later I still have times when I go back to counselling to talk about challenges that arise. Supportive relationships where speaking out is accepted and encouraged are in most cases often found outside the family, as disclosure of abuse to family often leaves the survivor ostracised and isolated without support.

At the time, talking about my abuse did not make me feel good, but over time it worked out to be the best decision I made. Because I have reaped the benefit of that positive choice, I no longer feel fearful about my future and so am no longer a captive to my past; I am free because in facing it I found my voice.

This is why I encourage you to release your secret. Secrecy is damaging on so many levels. The burden of secrecy affects inner peace, mental health, self-esteem, relationships and much more. Soon after my own abuse started, my dad told me if I ever told anyone what he was doing to me I would go deaf, dumb and blind. I remember feeling scared and bewildered that such a thing would happen to me, especially when I did not know what he was doing. Over the five years he was abusing me, I started not to care for the consequences. Being deaf, dumb and blind seemed a small price to pay to be free from my dad touching me anymore, and I was willing to pay it. Maybe it was defiance or being desperate to be free that led me to take a risk. I sometimes wonder if I had been older or didn't have the personality that I had, if I would have kept the secret; I am thankful I had the courage to make such a bold decision.

In today's society, more than ever options are available for you to disclose your secret. Are you someone that has lived with your secret for so long that you have become used it? Maybe you never felt safe enough to tell anyone. Were you threatened to keep quiet like me? Told no one would believe you or that you would be the one in trouble if you told anyone? Well look at me. I was told I would become mute, deaf and blind but guess who is here today speaking out raising awareness and educating people around the world on this issue? Me. Threats are only ever meant to keep you in the bondage of fear and give the abuser control. You can be free of this prison but it is a choice only you can make. If you choose to be free of the secret, you could do so at first confidentially. There are helplines that you can call and not have to give you name if don't want to. Breaking the silence is your first step to reclaim your life. Take the first step and see where it leads.

THOSE YOU LOVE MAY NOT SUPPORT YOU

92

I never received any support from my birth family. At the time I was angry and depressed about being ostracised from my family and did not expect to be accused of being a troublemaker or encouraged to go and apologise to my dad for the upset caused to HIM; I have paid the price for speaking out and standing in truth. Even with the lack of support, I do not regret speaking out. Something bigger was at stake than their support or approval; this was about my survival. It was about being free from the person that was hurting me physically, mentally and emotionally: my dad.

People believe blood should be thicker than water but unfortunately, I found this was not the case. If you have been fortunate to have family support after disclosing abuse that is a wonderful thing and hopefully those relationships will help you in your recovery from abuse. However, for those who have not had the support, it is a painful betrayal that many survivors never get over. I had to accept the loss of relationships with my birth family and I have managed to move on with my life. I did grieve for the loss but I am a better person for staying true to myself and choosing not to live a lie by having a relationship with them.

If you are in this situation, there may be a time after the rawness of your situation has died down that you may want to have a heart to heart with your loved ones if you feel this might help you on your journey to closure. My only advice to you is don't seek their acceptance to believe what happened to you as your foundation to heal and move on. You do not need anyone else's validation of your experience because you are the one who has lived with its aftermath. Do not let people manipulate you by using your vulnerability as a bargaining tool for acceptance and love. You can get support and be yourself without compromising your truth. Finding a good support network can make all the difference. This is why I set up Daughter Arise, an organisation that provides peer support and empowerment. Support can be found amongst others that have had similar experiences and by creating your own support network. I have created my own support network that includes my husband, a couple of trusted friends, other survivors and first and foremost my relationship with the living God. He has been my father and mother and been there in my time of need; he has never rejected me. (*Though my mother and father forsake me, the Lord will receive me – Psalm 27:10-14)*

HEALING IS A JOURNEY

A dear friend who had seen my struggles for a long time once said to me, 'Yvonne, do you realise the damage done to you during those five significant years of abuse could take five, ten years or even the rest of your life to undo?'

As a young woman in my twenties still struggling to grasp the enormity of the damage done to my life, I did not appreciate this comment back then. I was battling depression and struggling with showing myself compassion and understanding as to why it was hard for me to do certain things. I wanted to be healed, like yesterday! I was fed up with how this abuse invaded my life and wanted it out. I did not want to go back to therapy for what I felt like the hundredth time. I wanted to feel normal.

Reflecting on that conversation a decade later, I understood what she was trying to say. My friend, herself a survivor of childhood sexual abuse, was sharing her wisdom and experience of a realisation she made on her own journey. I was looking for an instant solution, a quick fix to a life-changing experience. As I have grown in wisdom and maturity on my own journey, I understand that I am made up of emotions and feelings, a soul and spirit that has been damaged and impacted by a traumatic assault inflicted upon my very being, and that needs time to heal. Yvonne needs time to heal.

On this journey to healing, I have cried so many tears and had to face fear head-on. I have had to learn what love is; what boundaries are. I have had to learn to forgive others and to forgive myself for my poor choices and mistakes that I have made (still trying!). I have had to learn what patience is and learn a different mindset in order to be free from destructive emotions that at times have kept me trapped in a vicious cycle. I had to learn how to treat others and me better (still learning!); I have learned to say no to behaviours that over the years felt good but were actually harmful to my well-being. I also came to the realisation that those who hurt me deeply care nothing for my pain. I have purposely made a choice not to sit and fester in anger about their disregard of my feelings and I

94

have let their offence go. Each day, month and year, I can say with confidence that I have not allowed my past to define me. I measure how far I have come by the outcome of the choices I made. Even when I have down days, I count them as part of the process of me finding myself and healing from my past.

You may not see now how you will make it through the pain because maybe like me you have a tendency to look at your faults, weaknesses or fears, but no one is perfect. I encourage you to lift your head up. Be kind to yourself for you have been through a lot. Be patient with you and do not let anybody make you feel bad that you are not at a place where they think you should be. It takes time to first admit what has happened to you and then to deal with and process all that it entails; it is hard. The journey to healing is one of a lifetime and the things you find hard now will get easier with time, and then you will find there will be different challenges that arise along the way. You have the power to determine how your past abuse will have a hold on the rest of your life. Do not look at your tears, anxiety or inability to embrace certain things now as indicators that you are not healing or making progress. In time, you will rise up victorious. I understand what it feels like to want to be rid of pain and disappointment, desiring in its place peace to live the life you want to live now, but it is a process. Do not be frustrated with yourself; everything will naturally happen in due season. (*Everything happens at the right time and season –Ecclesiastes 3:3*) Just do what you can with courage and the rest will follow.

YOU ARE WORTHY OF LOVE

As I say this to you, I continue to say this to myself: you are worthy of love. Real love does not harm or use our vulnerabilities against us. (*Love is patient, love is kind. It does not envy, it does not boast, it is not proud. It does not dishonour others, it is not self-seeking, it is not easily angered, it keeps no record of wrongs – 1 Corinthians 13:4-5*)

Real love is accepting of your faults and failings, and people that give it understand that you need time to learn, grow and heal. It is this kind of love that encourages you to keep on when you believe all hope has gone. I never experienced this kind of love until Jesus found me at 21 years old, and even when I have rejected his unconditional love and acceptance of me so many times, he was and is still faithful. I searched for so long for this type of love and acceptance from people but only found rejection and disappointment.

I often wondered why my parents could not give me this kind of love but after my therapy at 22 years old I came to the realisation: how can they give what they do not have? My first example of what love was supposed to be and how it was given was through my parents. Their example of love showed me it was to be betrayed, used and exploited. My dad used his love and my vulnerability as a child to exploit me; this distorted my ability to understand love. All the relationships I had from an age where I had freedom to make a choice were abusive to me. I believed sex was a tool to get what I wanted, but even then, I could not get the one thing I really wanted: love. I could not comprehend it because I did not know what it entailed. Promiscuity will not get you love because abusing yourself is not love. God says the spirit of love does not destroy. (*But the fruit of the Spirit is love, joy, peace, forbearance, kindness, goodness, faithfulness – Galatians 5:22*) It has taken the love of God to show me my value and worth through a personal relationship with Jesus, through his word the bible and by the examples of people who have shown me love in action in my life.

Slowly, I have accepted that I am worthy of love and I am learning to respond to it without lashing out or pushing it away. The negativity of my past from a young age told me that I was damaged and spoiled goods; that no one would love me. I choose now to embrace the truth: I am loved and I am a valuable child of God. The legacy left behind by my parents' so-called 'love' left me feeling I was of no value at all. Now I know I am fearfully and wonderfully made (*Psalm 139:14*). I am cared about, I am of value, I am not a mistake and that is the truth. This discovery of truth is not based upon what I think or feelings that are ever changing. It is based upon what my Heavenly Father says through his word, the bible and the revelation he has given me through our personal relationship. God says the same about you too.

These words of truth I have used as the foundation to build my new identity, alongside therapy; positive words of affirmation that I speak over to myself, learning about and accepting and loving me for who I am. No matter what has happened to you, no matter

96

how you feel about yourself, you are worthy of love; worthy of happiness and worthy of a good future that is not defined by the effects of your past. You may have to let some people go; you will have to let go of abusive habits and relationships in order to be at a place where an atmosphere of self-love can be nurtured and developed. It was after I got rid of abusive relationships and behaviours that it was the most difficult to believe I was worthy of love because I felt alone. After a while, whilst working on myself, I discovered the personal benefits of letting it all go, starting anew and not continuing the inheritance of my lost childhood. You may not believe it now but one day on your journey you will see the benefits of realising your worth; you are loved.

◆ EMPOWER POINT

Consider calling a confidential helpline for survivors of abuse. You do not have to give you name. Find out the name of a helpline that you could call. Write it down.

• **Have you ever attempted to tell anyone what has happened to you?**

• Do you blame yourself for what has happened? Why?

• What is your biggest concern about speaking out?

• If you have kept it a secret, have you found it beneficial?

• Is there a particular truth you have found true on your journey to healing?

(DIARY ENTRY – NOVEMBER 8TH 2000)

I feel quite low tonight, because since being here I've realised that I am very, very angry, but I do not know what with anymore. I feel scared about my future but I'm prepared to do whatever it takes to channel into myself to be me. To love myself and to believe in myself and not judge myself on what other people see.

(Written during stay at Charter Chelsea Clinic)

INTERNALISING EMOTIONAL PAIN

Besides being sexually abused as a child, I was abused emotionally, verbally and physically by a boyfriend I had in my teens. I subsequently ended up pregnant by him at 17 years old. The abuse I experienced at his hands left me broken and hurt and only served to further validate my belief that I was unlovable. I became worn down by the daily battles I had with him and his destructive need for control. I did not feel it was acceptable to just be me and, emotionally, I just gave up. The abuse I experienced in my life left me without a voice and had a negative impact on every aspect of my life especially in the area of forming healthy balanced relationships. The confidence to set boundaries with people was a complete challenge as I did not know how to assert myself. On reflection, I saw how I ended up in this relationship as a young vulnerable teenager. Low self-esteem, lack of self-love and a troubled upbringing left me looking for affirmation and acceptance in the wrong places. I searched for my identity in friendships and relationships that in some form allowed people to control me. I no longer had the strength to voice how ill treatment by people that I loved affected me, so I internalised my emotional pain and it affected my life in the following ways:
- Self-harming
- Anxiety
- Destructive behaviour (reckless choices, drugs, alcohol)
- Depression
- Anger
- Mental health issues
- Emotional numbness
- Excessiveness

Besides these issues, outwardly I continued to make poor relationship choices, struggled with parenting and my general outlook on life was very negative. In a workshop that I created and delivered to other survivors of childhood sexual abuse to help them explore finding their voice, they described how internalising pain affected them:

- Violence
- Sabotaging relationships
- Low self-esteem/low confidence
- Suicide attempts
- Self-pity
- Addictive behaviours
- Isolation
- Identity issues
- Negative self-talk
- Minimising abuse suffered

In a discussion after the workshop, the ladies came to the conclusion that it was good to talk about how they internalised their emotional pain, and for those of us that were able to voice suggestions, it was helpful.

◆ EMPOWER POINT

Have you internalised emotional pain? How has it affected you? In the space below write down in your own words what you have recognised?

(DIARY ENTRY – NOVEMBER 11TH 2000)

I just had support group and I feel quite angry. It is starting to come out and I don't know how to deal with it. I feel like physically punching something. Now I've swallowed it again, what will happen if it comes out?
(Written during my stay in Charter Chelsea clinic – 1st nervous breakdown)

EXPRESS YOURSELF

Thankfully, I now have a better understanding of how my experience of childhood sexual abuse influenced all aspects of my life, including relationship choices. But as a naive 16-year-old girl with low self-esteem issues, I rationalised that my ex-boyfriend's physically and verbally abusive behaviour towards me was not abusive when compared to the sexual abuse by my dad. The definition of abuse means to 'misuse, mistreat and handle with cruelty' so by this definition my ex-boyfriend was abusive in his treatment of me. Measuring one abusive experience against another only served to trivialise my pain and corrode my self-worth even further.

If you have been through emotional abuse, neglect and/or physical abuse, this also falls under the definition of 'abuse'. It was no surprise that after years of dealing with abuse and emotional trauma I had two nervous breakdowns in my twenties. The analogy of the bin which I explained to you earlier is something I now use as a visual aid in my workshops to show the participants how holding in harmful emotions and using unhealthy coping strategies can end up overwhelming you mentally and emotionally to a breaking point.

Besides the mental and psychological effects abuse can have on a person, it has been proved that trauma and stress can manifest themselves within the body in the form of physical ailments. When I was 24 years old, I went through a period of experiencing pain and weakness down the left side of my body. I had to go to the hospital for various tests including a full body scan, blood tests and neurological scans. After months of tests, the doctors could not find anything physically wrong with me but said stress caused by dealing with traumatic life events and other factors were likely to be the cause of my condition. Over time, with counselling, prayer and learning stress management techniques, the symptoms dissipated.

Studies have shown health issues such as unexplained fatigue, headaches and joint pain can be linked to trauma caused by childhood sexual abuse, and without proper medical investigation it would probably not be factored as a possibility that previous trauma could be the root cause of the problem. Internalising emotional pain can cause problems, but in taking steps to release it, the overall quality of your life will more than likely improve and some benefits may include:

- Less depressive episodes;
- A better outlook on life;
- Better physical health and fewer ailments;
- Increased self-esteem and confidence;
- Improved mental health.

Finding and expressing your voice is about you regaining power over your life. Ill treatment by others can lead to feelings of powerlessness and low self-worth. No matter how you feel about yourself, you are loved and valued by God. He knows the pain you are feeling and has kept track of your heartache and tears. (*He has kept track of your sorrows and collected all your tears in a bottle; he has recorded them in his book – Psalm 56:8*) Whether you believe it or not, God cares for you and wants to heal and restore you in a way you have never known, and that includes helping you find your voice. The first steps in starting to find your voice are the hardest steps to take and it is important for you to get support if needed to identify what has kept you from doing so. What hindered me from finding my voice was fear of judgement, abusive relationships and not trusting anyone because I had been hurt so deeply before. I started my journey to re-find my voice by:

- Getting help from mental health services (psychotherapy helped immensely);
- Keeping journals (have done so since the nineties);
- Attending support group (whilst in mental health clinics);
- Talking to confidential helplines (Samaritans, prayer lines, helpline for victims of abuse);
- Writing letters to self to encourage me, and outlet letters to people who have hurt me, to get out inner frustration (just as a release exercise, not to send);

- Writing my autobiography, 'Daughter Arise';
- Reading my bible, especially the psalms – (comforting during hard times);

These outlets have helped me at different stages of my journey and I still use the majority of them as and when I am in need.

◆ EMPOWER POINT – WHAT HAS HELPED YOU TO EXPRESS PAINFUL EMOTIONS?

List some outlets that have helped you during times of emotional pain.

• Have you found your voice? If you have not, what would help you to?

◆ EMPOWER POINT

If you have not listed any, don't worry! This exercise is simply trying to help you explore options that may help you through tough times. What outlets would you consider trying? Try to imagine no constraints, fears or obstacles of any kind!

MY LETTER TO SELF

February 24th 1999

Dear Yvonne,

I've been meaning to write to you for a long time now. I guess I have been putting it off. Actually, I have been scared of confronting you. You are a little girl who has never understood what happened to you. You just want to feel loved and secure, to be able to accept that you were abused and more importantly accept that you are worth loving and accept that you are who you are. Look in the mirror and see the person that God called to be his own. Yvonne, what happened to you wasn't your fault. You were a young child who trusted her dad and he took that trust and used it for his own evil ends; you were pure, just a child. I know you are fighting a constant battle with the ghosts that won't let you rest, you want justice, a feeling of vindication. A confession from your dad, admitting what he has done, and the fact that he calls you a liar and says your evil makes the rage and anger burn more. But Yvonne I feel you have a sense of the right direction. You need to believe in yourself and in what God tells you. I know you feel forgiveness of him is a no no but God says to forgive, because he forgave you and in order for you to move on you need to do this. You have got a lot to give but also let people give to you and don't push them away. Those barriers that are up now represent bitterness, hate and sadness so something has to give. Think about it.

Yours Truthfully

Yvonne

The first major outward step I took in finding my voice and expressing painful hidden emotions was an exercise called letter to self. Writing this letter allowed me for the first time to sit and reflect upon the damage caused by sexual abuse and to take stock of where I was emotionally, mentally and spiritually. I did this letter after I left hospital whilst recovering from a nervous breakdown as part of an exercise my psychotherapist set for me to help me get to know my inner self. I was able to take what I learned from this exercise to help me go forward to write more openly in my journals.

◆ EMPOWER POINT – LETTER TO SELF

I would like to encourage you to use this space to write a letter to your inner self. What would you say to your inner child? What encouragement would you give? The purpose of this exercise is to start to give you the space to find your voice. You may find on reflection it gives you more of an insight into yourself and a new perspective. This letter is purely for your benefit and you do not have to share it with anyone.

LETTER TO FAMILY MEMBER

March 1st 1999

Dear Mum,

I thought I'd write you a letter as there are many things I want to say to you. Ever since I came to your house 3 weeks ago, I had not heard from you, then when we meet up on Saturday, you did not have a word to say to me about what happened. It is as if you think by ignoring the situation it will go away; well it won't.

I know you're used to sweeping things under the carpet at the cost of us your children but you cannot see how extremely angry each of us have been at the way you have centred your whole world around that man. You probably think I went out of my way to cause trouble but I did not. He was saying some out of order things about me which you didn't say was not true. You stand there and let him say whatever he likes just to keep the peace; well, I ain't frightened of him and told him exactly what he is. He is the type of man who likes women to be totally under his control, to pander to his every whim and command. You are so desperate to stay with him that you cannot see how damaged all your kids are. He says he will leave you just to get you upset and because you want him to stay no matter what he does, even when he abused me for five years and couldn't answer the question, so basically what you're saying by staying with him is that it was alright for him to ruin my life. You won't confront him; he has a hold over you.

I cannot live a lie, just like I did before I left the house at 13. I will not live a lie to suit you or him, what he did to me was absolutely horrendous, I confronted him as you told me to and you know the truth so you have no more excuses anymore and I cannot be around you anymore knowing I did this and you thinking we can carry on pretending in our barely mother-daughter relationship; it can't happen. I do not think we should see each other again. I feel extremely let down in the way you have been with me since a child. You have been great support materially but it is not enough anymore. I am truly thankful for the things you have given me.

I do love you but you are destroying me.

Love Yvonne x

◆ EMPOWER POINT – YOUR WAY YOUR SAY

Using the following blank pages write, draw, create a poem or use art materials to express your feelings about how the actions of others have affected you. This exercise is about empowering you, enabling you to voice your experience. Find a quiet space or put on some background music whilst you do this exercise. Take your time. This is your ideal moment to start the journey of letting go of the past on your terms. You do not have to share this with anyone but if you want to reflect about it afterwards with someone it is your choice.

GOODBYE

Another exercise I found empowering was creating a goodbye bottle. There were many things I blamed myself for, including the actions of others against me. I held onto a lot of hurtful memories and this created a spirit of unforgiveness. In 2002, I wrote down on pieces of paper all that I wanted to let go of and put them inside a bottle that I took down to the Thames River at Battersea Park and dropped it in the water! Probably not the most environmentally friendly approach but at the time, watching it drift away gave me hope that I could put the past behind me. It was a symbolic visual reminder of what I was going to do through therapy, and by expressing myself through writing I started to let go.

◆ EMPOWER POINT – GOODBYE BOTTLE

What is the one thing you really want to say goodbye to? Is it a feeling, reaction or past behaviour? Is it to blaming yourself for other people's actions towards you, or blaming yourself for your abuse or past hurts that still affect you greatly?

The goodbye bottle signifies things that you are choosing to let go of whilst working towards embracing your new future. If you prefer, you can rip up pieces of paper and flush them down the toilet or make a small bonfire in your garden if you have one. The main aim is to choose a visual act that signifies you saying goodbye. Mentally and emotionally it will take time to catch up with the visual of the physical act you have done but that is okay; everything will fall into place in time.

PART FOUR – SUPPORT

(DIARY ENTRY – JANUARY 5TH 2000)

I'm determined to put the past behind me. I feel quiet inside, not depressed today. I am thinking about me and my future. I have to turn my life around. I don't need sex, it doesn't feel like it used to. Maybe it is because I am working through my problems.

SUPPORT AVENUES I HAVE TRIED

In order to disclose the secret, find your voice and withstand any accusation or issue. Support is not only important in going forward on your journey to healing from past trauma but is the underpinning that will keep you pressing forward with hope when you feel discouraged. Along my journey over the last thirty-three years, I have been helped and supported in various ways. I have participated in different types of therapies, attended abuse support groups, called phone helplines and had support from friends and other survivors. All of this support has helped me to get to where I am today and all served their purpose in helping me better understand who I am as a person. I want to share with you what support avenues I have tried and comment on what helped me as a female survivor.

• **Psychiatry**: I had psychiatric help after I was diagnosed with PTSD (post-traumatic stress disorder) at 13 years old and in my twenties before I was admitted to hospital with a breakdown. Psychiatry diagnoses mental health conditions and the psychiatrist can also prescribe medication and/or refer to other professional services for appropriate treatment. I found these sessions were more question type in approach and a stop-gap service whilst waiting to be referred onto other mental health services.

• **Psychotherapy**: This therapy gave me the tools to start the process of dealing with my emotions and exploring who I was for the first time in my life. Psychotherapy helped me deal with issues such as setting appropriate boundaries in relationships and other problems I found particularly challenging in the aftermath of sexual abuse.

• **Cognitive Behavioural Therapy (CBT)**: I used to have a negative outlook on life and always thought that any situation or bad thing that happened – problems in relationships or situations – was because of me, even when things were outside of my control. CBT helped me to take a step back to look at situations, to examine the source of my thoughts and gave me the tools to handle my emotions and look constructively at alternatives to the situation. I did CBT in my early thirties for around ten months. I found this helpful because mentally I was stuck in a negative mindset and some of the exercises I learned I still use today.

• **Counselling**: Referred through my doctor. Waiting lists for this type of counselling (listening only) can take up to six months and it is free in England on the NHS (National Health Service). After an initial telephone assessment, I was allocated to a counselling provider. I have used this service a few times over the years and each stint only lasts twelve sessions. It consisted of me talking whilst the counsellor listened. It was non-directive and I found it did not help me resolve my issues but was helpful to offload and express frustrations and difficulties. On the NHS, unless you are under a mental health professional, this is generally the first service they refer you to.

• **Medication**: I was first introduced to medication after my first breakdown. I was taking three different types of medication – Zopiclone, Olanzapine and Fluoxetine for depression, anxiety, insomnia and other issues. I did not like being on medication. I would get violent tremors, sweat profusely, was weak and tired most of the time and found it hard to concentrate. I did also try natural remedies such as St. John's wort but I did not find it effective either. I was 22 years old when I was put on medication and was taking tablets for two years. This was my experience – it may be different for other people.

• **Support phone helplines**: I have used them in emergencies on an as and when basis. There have been times when I have felt down or had an issue on my mind that bothered me and at weekends this avenue, which was the only option available, proved a lifeline. At

120

first, I would ring anonymously but then felt comfortable to give my name and the helpline operator would just listen and have a general talk with me about the situation. I have found Samaritans to be really good as well as helplines specific to my faith – premier prayer line and United Christians Broadcast helpline. They not only offer a listening ear but prayer as well. I found helplines to be a good avenue of support and immediate help.

• **Self-help books**: I haven't really come across many self-help books that deal with sexual abuse issues but in all honesty, the ones that I tried I found hard to read. The couple that I did buy and read had good information on the background of sexual abuse and its effects and did offer some self-help techniques on how to deal with issues, but I wanted something that was more rounded. What I wanted from a self-help book was a mixture of experience, awareness, education, empowerment, declarations, affirmations and exercises; a book that took you into the past but empowered you in the present to give hope for the future. Admittedly, I did give up halfway through these books. This was just to do with what I was looking for to help myself at the time. I did have an affirmation book that was given to me as a present during my stay in hospital from my nervous breakdown and I found it helpful because it focused not on the past but gave encouragement for the woman I hoped I would become.

• **Support group**: I have found support groups empowering and helpful. Attending support group whilst in the hospital recovering from a nervous breakdown in my twenties helped me to realise I was not alone, and being amongst like-minded people encouraged me to explore my voice. Now as a support group facilitator with Daughter Arise since 2014, I still find it empowering to be amongst other survivors to support them and be a part of their journey in the group. We all share in the group's success, and being able to hear what does or does not work has helped me guide the vision of the group in the right direction. We share helpful tips, ideas or current struggles and I create sessions for the group. The only thing I have noticed about being part of a support group is that you have to be at a certain place within yourself to find the courage to attend. Because of the secrecy and the negative connotations surrounding sexual abuse, some women find it hard to attend because just being present means others know you have been through abuse. But I believe peer empowerment can play an important part in a survivor's healing process.

- **Specialist sexual abuse trauma counselling**: Unfortunately, this service is not available on the National Health Service. I think it is outrageous that the NHS has not commissioned the services of counsellors that specialise in this type of counselling for survivors of sexual abuse. As someone who has experienced complex issues in the aftermath, in my opinion, specialised counselling is needed. The times I went to my doctor for help I did stipulate that when he made the referral that the counselling provider would be someone who specialised in this area, only to be told they could not give specific details on my requirements because the referral system goes to whichever provider has sessions available. In order to get specialised counselling, I had to pay for it. It is not cheap – sessions can start anywhere from £45.00 upwards, but on the plus side I have found it to be worth the money! I had to make sacrifices in order to access this help and could only afford to go once a fortnight. My last set of therapy was with a Christian counsellor that specialised in trauma issues, spiritual issues with a psychotherapy background. I found it hugely beneficial and to have someone with knowledge in all aspects combined really helped me to make great progress.

As you can see, I have accessed different avenues of support and then some! It was good for me to explore, try and test different options as part of finding the support that best suited me. It was important for me to start taking control of my choices, especially in the area of counselling and therapies. I found it empowering and the whole process gave me the confidence to start making decisions in other areas of my life.

To build new relationships required trust and I found that un-nerving at times but once the relationship was established with the counsellor I felt comfortable to open up emotionally. I did have a bad experience with a counsellor over a decade ago and it did put me off seeking help for a long while, but over time when I was ready, I started the process of seeking support again.

I cannot advise you on what support avenues would best work for you but the only advice I can give is to ask questions and research the background of where or who you are seeking help from, especially in the area of face-to-face therapy, counselling or support groups. What is it that you want to gain out of the service that you seek? Does it require money? Is it easy to travel to? Does the organisation/person have experience in dealing with the issues you are requiring help for? It is important to arrange phone conversations and/or emails to find out information so you can be clear on what is being offered to enable you to make a decision. If they are professional in their area of expertise they will not mind you asking questions. If face-to-face options are not something you want to engage in at this point in your life, explore other avenues of support.

Support will empower you to make changes and provide hope in your life and having the right support should:
- Give you a sense of hope;
- Empower you to make choices about your own life rather than letting others take control and make choices and decisions for you;
- Help you to start to change your mindset;
- Encourage you to face your issues;
- Help you build self-esteem and confidence;
- Give you strength to face problems that may arise unexpectedly.

It is important not to look at all your challenges at one time or you will find the work it will take to address them overwhelming. Do not look at the enormity of your problems. Do what you can each day to try and help yourself, for that is how the battle and the war are won. (*Therefore, do not worry about tomorrow, for tomorrow will worry about itself. Each day has enough trouble of its own – Matt 6:37*) Brick by brick a wall is built. One day you will climb over your present challenges to experience a new perspective on life; doesn't that sound promising? It does to me. A future not defined by the past is a wonderful motivation to attempt to try.

◆ EMPOWER POINT – TRY A NEW SUPPORT AVENUE

I have listed several avenues of support that I have tried over the years on my journey to healing from abuse. Some I found really helpful others were not suitable for my needs. If you have not tried any avenues of support, would you consider trying one when you need it? Maybe my list could give you some ideas or you may have something you want to try. Write down your thoughts on seeking support. What, if any, are your fears? Is there anything that is stopping you from talking to someone when you feel overwhelmed? Write down the pros and cons of your preferred choice and see if that helps.

• **What are my thoughts on seeking support?**

• Am I fearful about seeking support? If so, my fears about seeking support are...

• I think I can overcome my fear by...

• What new support avenues would I be willing to try?

Support Avenue	PRO – I will give it a try because…	CON – I will not give it a try because…

TOXIC RELATIONSHIPS

Support is the foundation of recovery but all that work can be undone if you do not have the right people around you. If you have made the initial decision to break free from your past and attempt the journey to wholeness and healing, you will need to pay special attention to your relationships and the people you have around you at this point of your life. Personal relationships are an area in my life where I learned the biggest lessons. I have learned through naivety, trial and error that people will either hinder, help or try to destroy you. I personally believe surrounding yourself with the right people is not only essential to your mental well-being but also pivotal in helping you move on from traumatic experiences towards reaching your potential in life.

Have you heard the saying, 'Bad company corrupts good character?' or 'Show me your friends and I'll show you your future?' These sayings have a certain truth to them. I have not always got it right when it comes to relationships or friendships but I can now say with measured confidence that in essence, I know what the traits of a productive, loving and supportive relationship look like. A good relationship speaks for itself.

The ability to discern people is not something that happens naturally. Many people, especially those of us who have been through abuse or come from backgrounds where parental relationships were either abusive or dysfunctional have issues in this area. I believe what allows unhealthy relationships to thrive for all the wrong reasons at the core, stems from low confidence and self-esteem. Unable to believe we deserve the best in all areas of life, including how we allow others to treat us, often leads to affirming these negative inner feelings in outward choices we make in regards to whom we form relationships with.

I did not make the connection at first that my poor self-esteem and low confidence were at the root of my poor relationship choices. What I found in my early years of self-discovery at the start of my journey in stepping out from under the shadow of abuse from age 13 to 24 years old, was the people I had in my life at the time did not mind when I was down and depressed without direction or hope. I let myself become a dumping ground for any destructive and negative behaviour and most of my friendships and relationships depended on me being emotionally weak and broken. As soon as I became stronger and learned to stand on my own two feet I became a problem. I even had an ex-friend at the time tell me that I would never make it far in life without her! I was shocked to see how me making a decision to change my life for the good could cause offence and upset to so many people, yet when I was doing the worst things and behaving in a negative way this was not a problem.

I believe the reason was that it either made them feel they were better than me or because of the drama I sometimes caught myself up in, it made them feel they were rescuing me. My search for affirmation and acceptance led me down the path of seeking attention from the wrong people and my vulnerability left me open to allow people to use it as an opportunity to control me.

Looking back, I am not shocked at how I ended up in these situations. These relationships were not built on a foundation of equality and I take partial responsibility for allowing others to interpret my insecurity as me being of lesser value than them. Now that I am in a different place, mentally and emotionally, I make better decisions in regards to relationships. I am fortunate that God used these situations to bring me to a new place in my life; a place where I could choose a new beginning. He opened the door to a path of self-discovery, but I had to choose to walk through it. I had to make the decision; I could choose to continue to engage in toxic relationships with people who were not interested in seeing me prosper and grow into a productive and mentally healthy woman, or have courage and faith to pursue new positive relationships.

If you decide to get therapy as I did, you may find keeping hold of negative relationships will not marry well with your journey to self-discovery and healing. My mindset changed as I slowly envisioned a life free from my past abuse. It was hard to cut ties with the dysfunctional aspects of my life and start again, as I had no point of reference to work from. But over time with the right support and knowledge, I have learned how to build good relationships and boundaries with people. Time has allowed me to grow in wisdom.

I have walked away from relationships with my birth family, superficial friendships, dysfunctional boyfriends, bad-minded ex-friends and surrogate parental relationships. But in their place I have found a relationship with Jesus who has been the foundation of wisdom in me building new relationships. (*Anyone who listens to my teaching and follows it is wise, like a person who builds a house upon a solid rock – Matthew 7:24*) I have a loving husband, a few trusted friends and a confidant, all who love and support me, I have no regrets. Some people are only meant to be in your life for a reason or a season, and for me the season of toxic friendships and relationships is over.

So what does a toxic relationship look like? From my experience, it involves a continuous play by others on your shortcomings and vulnerability. If you have people in your life that always tell you, 'You will never change' or constantly remind you that you are always messing up, this is an indication they are not good for your life. If you are managing, however small, to make positive, productive steps in your life and they are critical of it, saying things like 'You think you're better than everyone else' or making you feel insecure about those positive changes instead of encouraging and congratulating you, it is not a good sign either. Other signs may include not wanting you to give up certain behaviours or lifestyles. If you are not interested in doing certain self-destructive activities anymore and those around you encourage you to indulge in the very things that cause you difficulties, it is time to review these friendships. Be careful of who you confide in and those people who prove themselves untrustworthy. You tell them something about yourself and they take that information and spread it to others. You can tell these types of people because if they chat other people's business to you, they are most likely doing the same behind your back. Life change involves making bold decisions and re-evaluating all areas of your life. Learning to choose healthy relationships is one of those areas that needs regular evaluating.

Negative people have a way of viewing everything as a problem and never offer solutions. They cannot champion your willingness to change or embrace new things because more often than not their own lives are not going well. You cannot allow these types of people to poison your hope or cloud your optimism, and by being around them, their toxic energy will start to affect you too. With relationships like these, regardless of your loyalty to them, whether family or friends, they will prove damaging to your healing journey.

One thing you need to realise in rising out of such relationships is it will cause friction. The image of crabs in a bucket comes to mind as people who are not doing anything productive with their life will want the same for you too. You may find after making the decision to break free of them that you feel lonely or lost – you may even regret parting from them for a time. But in the long run, you will reap the benefits if you are willing to face the challenges and un-comfortableness of the short term.

New friendships can be found through getting involved in new interests and hobbies where you can meet new people. Joining support groups like Daughter Arise, you can find support amongst people who have had similar challenges, or like me, you can find faith and hope in a relationship with Jesus. He will give you peace and confidence to connect with people who will support and give you the courage to change your life.

Questions you should ask yourself about the relationships you have in your life are 'Does this relationship encourage, strengthen or challenge me or help me grow?' 'Do I feel comfortable with the dynamics of the relationship?' 'Is this relationship helping me to become productive in making positive changes in my life?' People who are for you will not feel threatened by your potential and willingness to better your life and will want to celebrate your success.

It is important to remember this is a lifelong learning process and that forging new friendships – even counselling ones – takes time. If you have rekindled friendships from the past, remember the person they knew back then is not who you are now. So if that person is reminding you of how you used to be at every opportunity, you need to ask yourself the question, 'Is this person part of the vision I have for where I am going in my life?' Be careful who you bare your inner feelings and thoughts to, and build relationships that encourage and help you grow as an individual.

◆ EMPOWER POINT – TOXIC RELATIONSHIPS

Are there relationships or friendships in your life that you recognise as toxic?

• What do you think would help you to break ties with these relationships or do you think they can be turned around?

- **Write down a statement for and against to argue the point of one of these relationships.**

For:

Against:

(DIARY ENTRY – NOVEMBER 23RD 2000)

I keep trying to grab onto things in my life. It feels sometimes that if I don't I will drown in all my emotions. I want to do something positive in my life, something new. I know what I need to do; start to enjoy my life and hold steady. Hopefully my emotions will heal and the wounds of rejection will repair.

DEALING WITH DIFFICULT TIMES

I always found night times my most difficult and vulnerable time. This is when I would either mix back with people I was trying to break away from or indulge in destructive behaviour such as smoking weed or self-harming. Over time, because I recognised a pattern of when I was most vulnerable, I started to put an action plan in place from the tips I learned from therapy sessions.

Loneliness is one of the biggest obstacles any human can face and as someone who has experienced it in the context of being ostracised by family in the aftermath of abuse, I can understand why some survivors would rather live with dysfunctional and destructive relationships rather than be by themselves. As soon as I entertained being in the presence of certain people, it always led to a slippery slope of regret; a cycle of self-blame and being hard on myself for not being strong enough to keep away from them. I did not know anyone at that point in my life that was on the same journey to encourage me, so when I became a born-again Christian, over time Jesus helped me to get through those difficult times. Talking to Jesus is like talking to a good friend. I did not have to be perfect to come into his presence; I came as I was. He promised to be there for me in my time of need and helped me in my time of trouble. (*God is our refuge and strength, an ever-present help in trouble – Psalm 46:1*)

◆ EMPOWER POINT – DEALING WITH DIFFICULT TIMES

When are you the most vulnerable? Do you revert back to old coping mechanisms during this time? Use the space below to write down three things that can help you during these times. It could be calling a helpline, friend or watching your favourite film – doing something that will help take your mind off the initial situation. It is better to try and have a think about it now rather than waiting to see what happens.

• **I am the most vulnerable when...**

• Three things I can do that would help me cope when I feel like this are...

•People I could possibly turn to for support when I am having a difficult time are...

•Where could I access emergency support if needed?

EMPOWERING SELF THROUGH DIFFICULT TIMES

In Chapter two, I mentioned five key areas that I found difficult on my journey to healing. I want to share with you some tips that I used to empower myself through those hard times and some practical points you may find helpful to use.

DEPRESSION

Besides seeking access to relevant help from mental help services, I devised a routine to help me through the day. Everyday tasks seemed impossible whilst in the midst of my depression. Here is a snapshot of how I planned my day:

My routine list

(Functioning through depression)
> Give daughter breakfast
> Wash myself and daughter
> Take daughter out to play
> Post letters
> Spend 15 minutes devotional time and prayer
> Exercise for half an hour
> Drink 1 litre of water and take vitamins

Actively writing down a structured list helped me to keep focus on what I had to do each day and helped me through a mentally challenging time. Not only did I have myself to look after, I also had my 1-year-old daughter and husband to consider.

If you are struggling daily to do small tasks, you can use the following pages to help write a list to structure your day. Creating a routine is important – even if it is only managing one task a day at first it is still an achievement. If you have not been diagnosed with depression but think you may be displaying symptoms, it is important that you seek professional help for a proper assessment. You can also ask your doctor for information on mental health charities in your local area (MIND or Depression Alliance if you are in the UK) that may be able to offer additional support. It is important

138

to remember that developing a set routine does not come overnight so do not be hard on yourself if you have a setback. It took a while before I stuck to my routine, but it was key to helping me function through depression.

◆ EMPOWER POINT – PRACTICAL TIPS ON FUNCTIONING THROUGH DEPRESSION

Make a small list the night before of what you want to try and achieve the following day. You can use the following space to make your list.

My 'to do' list

Sunday:

Monday:

Tuesday:

Wednesday:

Thursday:

Friday:

Saturday:

• Try and aim each day to do something you enjoy, even if you find it hard leaving the house. Reading, knitting, exercising, doing a word search or crosswords are all ideas. Have some background noise on; listen to the radio if it helps. Write down things that you enjoy.

I enjoy doing:

I enjoy it because:

• Try and sit by the window, go in the garden if you have access to one or venture out for a walk to the park to get some daylight – this can do wonders for lifting your mood.

Things that lift my mood are:

• Try and have a conversation or interact with someone for 15 minutes a day. Even if it is just to check in with a trusted companion or friend or even call a helpline. Isolation makes depression worse – it is good to talk and not keep things bottled inside.

I can call:

REJECTION

Being rejected by someone you care about can be a completely devastating experience, especially when you have done nothing wrong. Denial, in my opinion, is the root cause of rejection in regards to disclosure of sexual abuse. Unfortunately, the truth can be hard for people to hear, let alone except, but one thing you must try not to do is blame yourself. Rejection of this nature can trigger a survivor to have negative feelings about themselves. Rejection made me feel like I was not worth loving or fighting for and greatly impacted my self-esteem. What I found helpful besides talking and coming to terms with the loss of relationships, was to tell myself positive things about me and do things that helped me to take my mind off the rejection. After a while I gained hope and strength.

◆ EMPOWER POINT – PRACTICAL TIPS ON HELPING WITH REJECTION

Speak or write positive empowering, encouraging words to yourself such as 'It will get better over time', 'I will not always hurt this way', 'I will become a stronger person because of this experience'. (Check out Chapter Five affirmations to help you get started.)

My Affirmations

• Take up a new activity or hobby to take your mind off things.
Trying something new is an excellent way to build self- esteem.

Hobbies or new activities I would like to try:

• Consider counselling or an alternative support avenue to help you through this difficult period. Having the space to talk to someone can really help.

What I would be willing to try:

PARENTING

I had a lot of self-doubt about my parenting. I have always felt that somehow, I am not quite up to the mark. It is hard when you have no example of how to be a loving supportive parent, and at one stage I was terrified I would make the same mistakes as my mum simply because we share the same genetics. I am still learning not to let my fears and insecurities that stem from my own abuse get in the way of my daughter's right to a normal childhood. Whilst I do not allow her to go for sleepovers, she spends time with her cousins on a regular basis and is allowed to go to some parties and participate in normal childhood activities that both me and my husband feel is appropriate.

When my daughter was a toddler (she is 12 years old now) I struggled with isolating myself, so I joined a Mother and Baby group that was held once a week at my local church. I enjoyed taking my daughter there as I got to meet other mums, and my daughter had time to play.

I embrace this truth: I am not my mum nor will I make the same choices she did on parenting me. We are two different people with different outlooks, attitudes and perspectives that have shaped our lives. If you struggle with this fear because of your own abuse, know that you can now make different choices to your parents and whilst parenting as a survivor can be difficult, you can play a big part in creating good memories for you and your child.

◆ EMPOWER POINT – TIPS ON PARENTING

Join a parenting group if you have one near you. These are good sources of support. If you do not have one near you, online parenting groups like mumsnet (in UK; may be equivalent in your area) have many different discussion boards on a variety of topics, so it might be worth checking them out.

Places I can get support as a parent:

◆ EMPOWER POINT

Try and spend quality time with your child each day. I spend time with my daughter doing different things. We have pamper afternoons, watch a film, go out shopping or just sit on the bed and talk. It is not about the amount of time, it is about quality of the time. Put away any distractions that may get in the way of this; you can always resume what you are doing afterwards.

Things I could do in my quality time with my child:

• Write down one thing you are proud about in your parenting and use this as encouragement to help you in other aspects that your find challenging.

One thing I am proud about:

ANGER

If there was one area I have found really challenging over the years, it was controlling my anger. I would go from 0 to 100 real quick and found it hard to respond to certain situations in an appropriate way. I found my anger stemmed from lots of things but I have learned now to channel it in a non-destructive way. I have a lot of energy, so exercise has been a good outlet to deal with anger and stress. Journaling and writing poetry have helped me express negative feelings and also therapy. If you have a temper or struggle with anger, it is important to find non-destructive outlets to channel it.

◆ EMPOWER POINT – DEALING WITH ANGER

Try exercise. Exercise is a good outlet for letting out stress and irritability.

Exercise I could try:

• **Talk to someone.** Talking is a good way to communicate how you feel and if you are struggling to identify where the root of your anger is coming from, you could seek help by going to your doctor. Your doctor can help you decide an avenue best for you to pursue or you can look on the internet to find self-help suggestions.

I have found the following that could possibly help me:

• Get creative. Writing/journaling are good avenues I have found to get negative emotions out. You could even do art drawings to express yourself. Think about a creative outlet you want to try and give it a go. You can use the following pages.

My creative space:

AND FORGIVENESS...

Is a personal choice we can choose to make. The power of choice is in your hands and I cannot tell you that you must forgive, neither can I walk you through the process. What I can tell you from my own experience is, in order to heal my soul I had to release myself from the burden of hatred I felt towards my dad. To forgive does not mean that you automatically forget, and to forgive is not for the person who caused you offence's benefit – it is for your own. God says if we want to be forgiven we must forgive. Sometimes people forgive instantly; others do not and for others it is a process. Forgiveness is an act, not a feeling.

Be kind and compassionate to one another, forgiving each other, just as in Christ, God forgave you – Ephesians 4:32

PART FIVE – BEAUTY FOR ASHES

(DIARY ENTRY – NOVEMBER 14TH 2000)

There has been a realisation within me; I know when I look in the mirror who I am and what I feel. For far too long I have portrayed myself as someone I am not and have spent so much time running away from self, because I did not want to believe who I have become. I did not want to believe that so many sad situations changed me into a jumbled-up wreck. Vivid images of good times saturated with bad, I could not separate my past from my present. Until now. I cannot live in the past, I can get over the pain and be someone, do something with my life and achieve. There is something great about me I can feel it; it just has not been realised and unleashed yet. I have never really wanted to die; I just wanted the suffering and disappointments to end – the memories of abuse, my mum's rejection, the pain caused by my ex-boyfriend, the abortion. It is hard to believe I am only 24 years old. Tonight I put all these things to rest; it is time to let go. Stress has been like a cancer in my life, slowly eating me up and wearing me down. I accept that a new life is ahead and I need not be afraid; I have made it this far, faith is with God.

REALISATION

It was a sobering moment when I realised the years spent trying to run from my problems was a waste of time. I was so tired of the pretence; so broken and hurt inside I felt like I was strapped in a straightjacket of emotional pain. In order to cope, I used whatever vice of choice would distract me from what I was feeling, but no amount of weed, alcohol and frequent episodes of self-harming could soothe my sadness or fix my broken reality. I had no inner peace and I was tired of the pretense of appearing normal when I just about functioned every day. I knew I had to let go of all that was holding me back, but how? I had no idea how to do this, as with my own efforts I had failed. The avenues I tried offered only the illusion of peace; that was until I got to know the Prince of peace – Jesus. (***Peace I leave with you; my peace I give you. I do not give to you as the world gives. Do not let your hearts be troubled and do not be afraid – John 14:27***)

It was through a relationship with Jesus that peace came into my life and the revelation of his love helped me to understand that my life was never meant to be this way. Unfortunately, I was born a victim of circumstance, born into an incestuous family with parents whose selfish needs outweighed their moral duty to me as their child; I never stood a chance. The realisation that I could be free from my past was both frightening and exciting at the same time, but it has been an everyday battle to choose choices that enable freedom in my life. It has been twenty years since I gave my life to Jesus Christ as a born-again Christian and ten years since I had the revelation that I could live a life free from the bondage of sexual abuse.

Do you know the pain, heartache and sadness you have suffered because of your abuse was never God's plan for you? I know. You may ask the question, 'How could God (if he even exists) allow me to go through such terrible circumstances if he loved me?' The truth is, I do not have the answer as to why any of us have suffered the abuse that we have. Sometimes in moments of vulnerability and upset, I still ask God why I was abused, and whilst I have never received an answer, I am content at this stage in my life knowing that all things that were meant for bad will be turned around for good. (*You intended to harm me, but God intended it for good to accomplish what is now being done, the saving of many lives – Genesis 50:20*). God has given everyone (that includes you and me) the gift of free will. People use their free will, (freedom to make right or wrong choices) to either help or hinder another person's life. Sexual abuse or any abuse, in my opinion, is the ultimate hindrance that someone can inflict on a child's life.

God is very clear in his word, the bible, that we should treat others how we want to be treated (*Treat others the same way you want them to treat you – Luke 6:31*) but unfortunately, the people we trusted have treated us appallingly. This is of little comfort or consolation when you have been betrayed and exploited by people you trusted, loved or cared for. In the aftermath of abuse, we are the ones left to pick up the pieces of our lives, more often than not facing the journey to recovery by ourselves. So many survivors suffer in silence because of fear and because what happened to them is too shameful to even acknowledge or mention. As survivors, we subconsciously take on the shame and burden of the perpetrators' actions with little thought to the damage caused to our well-being.

It, therefore, proves completely challenging to hear that God loves you; but you are precious in his sight. The wonderful thing

164

about God is his word is not based on feelings but the truth of who he is, and he does not lie. (*God is not a man, that he should lie; neither the son of man, that he should repent: hath he said, and shall he not do it? or hath he spoken, and shall he not make it good? – Numbers 23:19*) The irony is that in order to be free from your past you have to be the one to make the choice to want to engage in the hard work it takes to rebuild your life.

Life does get better but I can tell you even now, decades after my own abuse, I still experience times when I struggle to believe I am worthy of love and deserving of a good life. Every day I proactively engage in small steps to renew my mind by reflecting on my progress and being thankful for where I am today, and that helps me to keep everything in perspective. Considering all that I have been through, it is a miracle I have made it this far in life – not surviving but thriving. I affirm and encourage myself by writing and speaking positive words, quotes and poems, engaging in prayer and reading my bible daily because this is where the source of my truth and peace comes from. I have to make a choice in spite of feelings because left to my own devices, if I were to listen to my thoughts and feelings, especially on the days when I feel vulnerable, I would be totally convinced that I am worth nothing. The truth is both you and I are loved and cherished by God; we are not a mistake even though our insecurities and experiences try to convince us otherwise. (*You knit me together in my mother's womb, I praise you because I am fearfully and wonderfully made – Psalm 139:13-14*) God planned for us to be here in this world at this time; there is still hope for both you and me.

It is hard to fathom that the creator of the universe, the Living God would want to trade the ashes of your past (problems, abuse, difficulties, pain caused by others) for his beauty (victory, joy, peace, hope and a future) when you have lived with the devastation for so long and even resigned yourself to it. It is hard to believe life can get better, that you can feel positive about yourself and emotionally heal from your abuse. But I want to testify to you that I have experienced first-hand God's goodness in my life and that, in fact, he did indeed take my shame, burden and pain, and in exchange has given me his love, peace and his presence that has empowered me to turn past devastation from my abuse into life-giving purpose. Through his son, Jesus Christ, this restorative spiritual work has provided the healing to release me into a deeper understanding of who I am and given me a new outlook on life.

It is part of life's natural process to mourn for something we have lost but the grieving process is not meant to last forever. Being in a state of continued mourning will leave you emotionally, mentally and spiritually depressed and drained, and when you are in this mindset you cannot embrace or experience anything positive or life-changing in its entirety. There must come a time when you move past your abuse and engage and renew your mind with the knowledge that will help you work towards a new future.

RECLAIMING YOUR LIFE

At the beginning of this book, I shared with you a card my friend wrote to me about reclaiming my life. It was at this very stage that I was sitting in the ashes of the aftermath of my abuse. I re-lived every moment of my past in the present, I cried and mourned every day at the loss and injustice, and could not see a hopeful future for me. My identity was firmly attached to my past and no matter what my friend, herself a survivor of sexual abuse, shared with me as encouragement that life would get better I did not believe her. She would take me to Christian conferences, encourage and tell me that God loved me but I refused to believe it. Many years later, after gaining the courage to face my inner pain, I finally understood that in order for my life to change I had to first reclaim my life; even in its broken state my life was still mine and no one could take my present and potential future away from me.

As I took the steps to reclaim my life, I was like a new-born baby, learning things for the first time. I had to learn how to accept help, make difficult choices, seek the right knowledge so that I could break my negative mindset, and let go of destructive habits. I had to make tough decisions at every turn in my life, sometimes having tantrums of resentment about having to do the work involved but Jesus walked me through every stage and put people around me to support and help me.

I know women and men that started the journey to make positive steps in reclaiming their life after childhood sexual abuse. They did well to move away from toxic family situations, stop engaging in dysfunctional activities only to knowingly sabotage their own progress because things were going too well. They actively hindered their progress because the chaos and dysfunction of their past were what they were used to and when faced with having to deal with their situations or emotions in a different way, would revert back to the old coping mechanisms they were familiar with.

The work of reclaiming your life involves thinking about your decisions and taking control of your choices rather than allowing the runaway train of dysfunction (just going through life accepting and doing whatever it takes at the moment in order to cope and get through) to cause more chaos and drama. Many survivors live their lives in survival mode. The problem is once out of the initial traumatic experience of sexual abuse, the coping techniques used to function in the aftermath do not fit into the journey of recovery.

I struggled with self-sabotage because I had low self-esteem. I would reinforce these negative feelings by going back and sleeping with an abusive ex-boyfriend over a period of seven years. When I felt out of control emotionally, I became reckless and made bad decisions based on my feelings. I knew it was wrong and destructive to be intimate with him but when those feelings of worthlessness arose within me, I validated them by going back to the one person who would negatively affirm this by the way he treated me. Self-sabotage is something as a survivor you need to be mindful of by developing an awareness of triggers within self that may spark you to go off track; this can be done with professional help. I learned to recognise my triggers from help through psychotherapy and cognitive behaviour therapy (CBT). Once you have made the decision to reclaim your life with the support, you can develop a strategy to help you.

You are not defined by your past and you certainly do not owe your past any more of your time and energy. Just because you have been left with the ashes of abuse does not mean those ashes deserve a place in your life now. Think about the image of ashes. What does it remind you of? Ashes by their nature represent something ruined, destroyed, never to be used again. The memories of your lost childhood and the promise of what could have been, are gone. Coming to terms with the fact that my childhood was ruined took me a long time to accept. I will never get back that period of my life to explore the potential of the young woman I was emerging into at that time. These are now part of my ashes that lay waste on the ground of what could have been but I do have an expectation of hope for a better future, exceeding my own expectations and living out my goals and dreams.

◆ EMPOWER POINT – TRADE FOR A TRADE

Imagine if you could trade emotional, mental or physical obstacles that hinder you moving forward, what would you trade them for? So, for example I might put in the first column, 'anger' and then in second column swap it for 'peace'. Below are three columns, one for the issue and the other for what you would like to have instead. The things that you list are relevant issues that are impacting your ability to move forward in your everyday life. Once you have made your list, write down in the third column what you believe it would take to achieve this in reality.

I would like to trade	For...	What could help make this a reality?

DO YOU WANT TO BE WELL?

Sometime later, Jesus went up to Jerusalem for one of the Jewish festivals. Now there is in Jerusalem near the Sheep Gate a pool, which in Aramaic is called Bethesda and which is surrounded by five covered colonnades. Here a great number of disabled people used to lie—the blind, the lame, the paralysed. One who was there had been an invalid for thirty-eight years. When Jesus saw him lying there and learned that he had been in this condition for a long time, he asked him, 'Do you want to get well?'

'Sir,' the invalid replied, 'I have no one to help me into the pool when the water is stirred. While I am trying to get in, someone else goes down ahead of me.' Then Jesus said to him, 'Get up! Pick up your mat and walk.' At once the man was cured; he picked up his mat and walked. (The Healing at the Pool – John 5 v 1-8)

Jesus asked the man this question because wanting to be well had to be a decision he made in spite of his predicament. This man lay at the poolside for thirty-eight years and had grown used to living in his condition. He had grown accustomed to living without hope, living with his past and present with no hope for a better future. Others around him tried to position themselves to get into the water to be healed, understanding that tenacity was required, yet this man was not able to get himself to that point and relied on others to get him in and out of the pool. When Jesus asked him the direct question of wanting to be well, the man, realising the importance of the moment, made a decision to take a step of faith and courage to get up.

I used to live in this state. For a long time, I would repeat my past life story to anyone who would listen so they would agree, that I had, in fact, been treated badly. This mindset was naturally birthed out of my being sexually abused and the deep sorrow and the injustice I experienced in life. I used it as an excuse not to apply myself to any process that required me to start the journey to healing or anything that challenged me to step out of my comfort zone. At the time I believed living this way was protecting me but it only hindered me going forward in my life.

Have you grown used to living with the hurt and issues that have stemmed from being abused? If so you don't have to live this way. You can start the process of being healed from your past just as I have. A relationship with Jesus can bring you healing and the help you need to overcome your past. If you are willing to take a step of faith, he will meet you at your point of need. Are you willing to try and trust him? If so you can pray this prayer:

Dear Jesus,

I would like you to help me as I am struggling with my past. Please can you take my pain, issues and trauma caused by the sexual abuse I have suffered and, in its place, give me your peace and joy. I am asking you to help me take the steps to be free of this and ask that you guide and direct me into true freedom. I believe you can help me. I believe you are the son of God and that you died so that I may experience everlasting life. Come into my heart and life that I may personally know you. Please put people around me that will help and support me as I cannot do it alone. I thank you that you have heard my prayer and trust that you will reveal yourself to me and deliver me from every stronghold in my life.

In your precious name Jesus. Amen

God gave his one and only son, Jesus Christ, in order that we may experience a new life. (For God so loved the world, that he gave his only begotten Son, that whosoever believeth on him should not perish, but have eternal life – John 3:16) This new life involves being spiritually reborn; being born again. (That which is born of the flesh is flesh, and that which is born of the Spirit is spirit – John 3:6) The regeneration starts from the spirit and transcends into the soul – thoughts, feeling and emotions. I came to experience this new life when I was well and truly at the end of myself, as I hit rock bottom. Everything I tried to forget my abuse did not work; people had given up on me and only tolerated me. I had no one I could turn to and was in despair from my troubles. It is said that when you are at the end of yourself, that is when you will truly find Jesus – I have found this to be true. I came to him as I was and my life has never been the same since. It may be hard for you to believe God cares about you, loves you and wants a personal relationship with you when you may feel he abandoned you in the first place. If you are willing to take a step of faith over time you will begin to reap and see the benefits of trusting in the Living God.

The point of the exercise, trade for trade, is that I want to show you that trading your sadness and disappointment for peace, hope and freedom is a reality if you trust Jesus. The pain I felt no longer affects me in the way it used to. Sure, the imprint of my past will always be there but it is a distant memory that creeps back now and then, not something that I keep reliving from a point of my actual reality. The best analogy I can give is that of a scar that has healed but the mark is still there. It is a living reminder of a past life event, not a festering open wound that is raw and painful to touch.

As with any relationship, a relationship with God will take time to build. Time, God willing, is the only thing we have on our side, and the liberty of being granted it teaches patience and allows the groundwork of relationship to be built. The same can be said for the process of overcoming issues and difficulties. God provides time and healing to complete the work of restoration and renewing our minds, using resources, people and his guidance to work for his glory and our benefit. No one can take the credit for the woman I am today apart from God, through his son Jesus Christ. His hand has guided all sources of help and support that have contributed to my transformation.

FORGIVE YOU

I struggled with forgiveness of self over the years and have a habit of giving myself a hard time for things in and outside of my control. I criticise myself now for choices I made when I was younger, from my position now as a woman in a better place in my life, which is not fair. I am slowly learning to have compassion for me and understand that it is okay to make mistakes; I am not perfect.

◆ EMPOWER POINT – FORGIVE YOU

Choose this day to forgive yourself for any actions, decisions or behaviour that you took to help you get through the pain of your abuse. Jesus forgives you. Confess to him all your burdens for he cares for you. (*Give all your worries and cares to God, for he cares about you — 1 Peter 5:7*). Please release yourself from whatever you have carried for so long. It is okay to let go and let God in. He can carry the weight of your pain, shame and despair because Jesus died to carry our sin. Write down the things you need to forgive yourself for and ask Jesus to release you from its burden.

I FORGIVE MYSELF FOR…

(DIARY ENTRY – MARCH 2000)

Yesterday I felt so muddled up and bewildered. The day started off really well, I felt Gods presence so strongly it was like a warm well bubbling up inside me. Instead of going back to bed after I dropped off my daughter, I came home and got dressed. As I was doing this I put on a lovely gospel tape, I felt really happy even though by the afternoon certain events happened. I feel hopeful because I am rediscovering my faith. Anyway, I went to therapy and boy, it was hard but it was worth it. I found myself opening up more than I've done recently in therapy. It left me feeling a little vulnerable but I realise in order to heal I need to go deep into my memory to reveal the things I chose not to remember and bring them out in the open. I feel so insecure and worthless at times, and when I feel like that I think all kinds of destructive things.

Sometimes I feel so angry at my treatment by others that I want to cut myself again with a razor, by God's grace I did not do it. One day God will release me from all the things that keep me in bondage. He is the most powerful force ever and I will try hard to cling to him.

REBUILDING THE RUINS OF YOUR LIFE

The work of rebuilding your life is a slow and delicate process that requires time, patience and endurance. As previously mentioned, I started this process at 22 years old – thirteen years after the initial abuse happened. Before work can begin, acknowledgement of what happened to you is the first step and foundation upon which everything else will be built. It is painful to have to face and admit it, but with time you will find that acknowledgement of your past will unlock doors within you that may have been deliberately or subconsciously shut.

In acknowledging the damage sexual abuse had caused in my life and working on the unresolved issues, my view of life and perception of who I was, changed. Up until this point, my identity was based on my own beliefs and feelings left behind from abuse. I had to learn a new mindset in order to embrace a new self in order to learn a new way of living.

On this journey to knowing self and rebuilding your life, deliberate choices and decisions must be made to fight against the coping mechanisms, behaviours and actions that have been comfortable for so long. In order to be equipped for the work involved, you will need to address every area of your life that has been affected and the majority of the work starts with your mindset. When your soul (mind, thoughts, emotions and feelings) are in a place of negativity, it leads to words and actions that affirm that negativity. I never gave any thought to the way I spoke about me and did not realise the connection between my negative words and actions, because my mindset was stuck in the past. I was physically free from the acts of abuse but I was not mentally free. The saying 'Knowledge is power' could not be more true. I had to gain knowledge about how to free my mind from the shackles of my past through many different channels – therapy, books on topics on healing from sexual abuse, building my confidence and self-esteem. Also, I listened to people speak about emotional healing and recovery, and the bible has provided the spiritual framework to make all this retained knowledge applicable to my life.

As the saying goes, Rome was not built in a day, and the same applies to rebuilding your life post-abuse. You will have good and bad days and there will be times when you might slip back into old habits for security or self-preservation. Factor this into the equation as part of the journey and do not be hard on yourself. It may take a long time to undo all the damage that sexual abuse has brought into your life; remember patience is key.

SELF-CARE

Self-care not only involves doing things that enhance your life in the long term, it is also about maintaining everyday aspects. It is not only mental health that needs looking after but also physical health too. I struggled with anxiety and depression for over twenty years and during those times my eating habits were dysfunctional. I remember just before I had my first nervous breakdown in my early twenties, I stopped eating completely because I was depressed and sad. It was not my first priority and it seemed like whenever I ate, food got stuck in my throat so it seemed better not to bother. Instead, I would smoke cigarettes and drink alcohol mostly on an empty stomach. When I did eat food, usually once a day, it would consist of junk – crisps, cake, nothing healthy or substantial. Because of my sporadic eating habits, I lost a lot of weight quickly. I was a size UK10, so imagine what I looked like! I was skinnier than I needed to be and looked drained. I understand how it feels when you are depressed and preoccupied with your troubles; emotional pain has a way of shutting down the body. Below I have put together a list of five areas that you should maintain.

Eat well: You may not feel like eating three meals a day but you could try things like protein bars, cereals, and fruit as on the go foods, or soups, salads or pasta as a main substantial meal. These foods have nutritional value that will benefit your body. You could also try making your own smoothies or buy them ready made. You may not have the energy to cook so, as a short-term solution, buy ready meals that can be heated up in the oven or microwave. Many supermarkets now have healthy options that consist of stuff that is good for you. Remember...this option is only good for a period of time until you get back on your feet. Try and have healthy snacks such as nuts, yoghurts or dips as snacks and have something small to eat every 3_4 hours. This will help keep your energy up and ensure your body gets what it needs.

Drink plenty of fluids: By fluids I do not mean alcohol! Drink plenty of water. It is recommended that you drink 2.5 litres a day. That seems like a lot, I know, but even drinking a litre a day is a start. If you do not like drinking plain water, try the fruit varieties or fruit teas and juices but avoid fizzy or caffeinated drinks. Keeping hydrated will keep headaches at bay. Water also helps with concentration.

Exercise: You only have one body so it is important that you look after it. I have always liked exercise, so that area of looking after myself was never a huge problem for me. Admittedly, it was after the birth of my second child that I started to take exercise more seriously than before; because I was not overweight I did not put in much effort! Exercise benefits the body internally as well as externally. It also was a huge major factor in reducing the episodes of depression I suffered for many years. Exercise releases chemicals in the brain called endorphins. These endorphins interact with receptors in the brain and trigger a positive feeling to the body; that is why doctors recommend exercise as an outlet for helping depression. I can testify to the benefit of exercise in this area and it has greatly improved all areas of my life. I am often told during my annual medical with my doctor that I have the blood pressure of a 16 year old! I take that as a compliment!

You do not have to go the gym or exercise four to five days a week like I do, but doing a little exercise each day to get the heart rate up is a good thing. If you do not like the gym, you could exercise in the comfort of your own home. YouTube on the internet has various different exercise videos that you can do – Pilates, cardio, weight lifting – there is a fantastic choice available. Fancy a change of scenery? How about taking a walk to the park or around your local area? You could take a brisk walk, power walk or jog; it is completely up to you.

It is recommended that you exercise half an hour a day, five days a week, but if that seems a lot, three to four times a week should suffice. It does not matter how you do it just as long as you are getting it done, so start moving!

Smears: One area I did not do so well in and continue to struggle with is smear tests. I hate them! Everything about them seems daunting to me and I identified the core of why I feel like this – I do not like feeling vulnerable. I feel helpless and out of control during the examination and the cold equipment they use only heightens my anxiety! I thought I was the only survivor who experienced these feelings until I researched on the internet and found not only female survivors of sexual abuse experience the same anxiety but also a large percentage of women in general, and they struggle to attend scheduled appointments as well!

It is a tricky situation but it is of the utmost importance that you go, as detecting abnormal cells early on with treatment can reduce the risk of cervical cancer. How I have dealt with attending smear appointments is by telling the nurse before my examination that I am a survivor of childhood sexual abuse. This helps the nurse to understand my anxiety and do the examination with more sensitivity. With each nurse I have had during my examination they always explain each step of the smear and even make small talk with me to

178

keep my mind off of it. I have kept up with my smears over the years – with hesitancy I eventually do them. If you struggle in this area you could try sharing with the health professional why you find smears difficult. They are bound by confidentiality so you do not have to worry about what you say being repeated. You do not have to tell them your whole life story but just say enough for the nurse to understand. You may also want to bring a friend or someone to support you when you go for your appointment.

Dental check-ups: Another area survivors find hard because of the element of vulnerability. The feeling of helplessness is enough to avoid dental check-ups at all costs. If you find this difficult, you can explain to the dentist why you are anxious and also ask someone to support you in attending this appointment. I was okay with dentist visits but that changed when I was 23 years old. The dentist needed to put in a filling and gave me an injection but the problem arose when he administered it and made several attempts at doing so. This caused me to panic and have anxiety. Now to go to the dentist, I have to have a big lead up to it in order to go. I now go to a dentist that is sensitive to anxiety issues and that has really helped. If you have problems in this area, I suggest you find a dentist this is sensitive to patients with anxiety around dental care.

Sleep: Worry, anxiety and depression can cause havoc with sleep patterns. I still at times experience problems with anxiety and stress and it has an impact on me getting to sleep. When I suffered from depression, I would sleep all day and be up all night. I would go to bed at 11 pm and by 1 am be wide awake. Lack of sleep affects concentration, ability to make thought-out decisions and depletes energy levels.

As I have dealt with sleep problems in one form or another over the years, I have found strategies to help me. For instance, having a warm bath before bed can help relax the mind and body. A warm drink – hot chocolate, milk or blackcurrant – may also help. Going to go to bed at a reasonable time even if you cannot sleep and turning off mobile phones, TV and social media is a good idea, as over stimulating the mind will keep it active when it should be preparing to switch into sleep mode. Instead, I recommend reading a book or listening to the radio on a low volume. Creating an atmosphere that inspires relaxation will help you to get to sleep. It may not happen straight away – I would go through periods of sleeplessness over two or three-week cycles and was extremely exhausted. My doctor suggested I try anti-depressants as a solution to help the problem but I have been hesitant in taking them again. I have used sleeping tablets but I do not like the hungover, groggy feeling that it leaves behind when I wake up so I tried alternatives such as Nytol, but I did not find them that effective. Prayer, focusing and meditating on God's peace helps me to relax. See what works for you and hopefully, over time, you will see some changes. You can always seek advice from your doctor for other options.

Emotional care (mental health): I believe one of the major keys to recovering from the trauma of childhood sexual abuse is finding an outlet to express inner feelings. As mentioned in the chapter 'Facing your past', internalising painful inner emotions can cause harm to your overall well-being. Any expressive activity – journaling, writing poetry, art or talking with someone – does have benefits that can greatly improve quality of life. It is important that you explore an avenue that best suits you and feel free to try new things. I know it may seem scary or feel hopeless to try, but I encourage you to give it a go. Emotional care also means having the right people around you to help you; people who have empathy and can help you overcome your challenges.

Self-care really is about appreciating and being kind to yourself. Do nice things for yourself. The journey to recovery from sexual abuse can have an effect on all areas of life so steps to self-care serve as vital rest stops on its uncertain road. My hope for you is that if you are not already investing the time in self-care that you make a start to.

◆ EMPOWER POINT – SELF-CARE CHECK LIST

If you have identified any areas of self-care that you are struggling with, write them down and write things that you are willing to try to help address this area in your life.

Self-care areas I struggle with:

What I am going to try to help in my self-care routine:

ABUSE TAG

(Poem I wrote in 2017)

It happened to me but it is not my identity
It was my past but it is not my present or my future
I was a product of its effects
But it only served to strengthen and build my character
It is a chapter in my life not my whole life story

People used it to try and box me in,
To harm me, to hurt me
It was their Ace card
They used to try to define and destroy me

The past was never the past, even though it was my history
The pressure to be what society expected me to be
With no parents, support, love or empathy
But no matter what it brought in the aftermath of its calamity
God has shown if he is for me. Who can be against me?

Daughter Arisen, Daughter Arise
No one expected me to do that, because the odds were stacked high
I am not the stereotype they expected from someone defiled as a child
They expected someone down trodden and forgotten
Mentally broken, addicted, angry and wild
Yeah, I was that woman for a while
But Jesus in his power transformed my life and because he conquered, I smile

I am not ashamed of that
I don't care how nerdy it looks
I lived the life, paid the price and wrote it in a book
And I am on a mission to show others you can escape its deadly hook

Society wants me to be quiet, survive and let life take its course
But I am on a mission to take back everything that was stolen from me, get

double for my trouble and more
With guidance from my powerful source
I will not only survive, I will thrive and exceed
I will do the things that people laughed in my face
And told me
I will only dream

The box that sexual abuse tried to build for me, has been broken wide
For under its guilt and shame I will not cry and hide
It is no longer welcome to dwell in my life
It was never a friend of mine

You can choose if you want it to stay
Not only in your yesterdays, today and rest of days
Or you can take the tag off that it has labelled and packaged you in
But it will take courage to face your past, find your voice and dare to live.

You can do exceedingly, abundantly and above all things
The hope that you think is lost, is nearer than you think
Look deep inside you and the key can be found
No matter what your family, people or society say
From this day, if you choose, your life can start on solid ground

By breaking the abuse tag
You can be free
To live the life you want
Built on a new identity

Yvonne

PART SIX – CHOOSE LIFE

(DIARY ENTRY – AUGUST 25TH 2000)

I dream that one day I will be confident and that I will be able to love myself and stand firm in God and trust him fully; that one day I will be rich and powerful not just materially but spiritually, and that I'll be married to a man who loves me for me.

DREAMS

I wrote these powerful words in my journal whilst I was recovering from a mental breakdown in hospital. As I looked out of my bedroom window, metal bars obscuring my view, I thought my life was over, but still a spark of hope was in my heart. I wanted so desperately to believe there was more to my life than my reality, because at the time my reality seemed so final. But look at me now. Here I am twenty years later – married for thirteen years, Founder of an organisation that supports survivors of sexual abuse, Author, TEDx speaker amongst so many other things. If someone told me all those years ago when I was in that hospital I would achieve all that I am have today, I never would have believed them. It just goes to show the power of words and hope. I chose to speak life into a dark place in my life not knowing those words have come into fruition.

So what does it mean to choose life? For me to choose life means to hope for and desire a better future not limited or defined by my past abuse or the mindset left behind in the aftermath, but from choices and decisions I can now make towards determining a better future for me. It is not easy to believe better things can happen in your life when life so far has left you depressed and broken, but I found envisioning a better life inspired me to have hope in spite of how my present life was. To choose life involves making hard choices and take deliberate actions when everything within you wants to give up. It means taking slow progressive steps, using supportive help tools along the way and understanding that it is neither the pace nor time it takes to get to your desired destination or outcome that counts; it is the effort that counts. To choose life means to embrace where you are now and accept that even with your flaws and insecurities you can still be the unique great person that you want to be and achieve your dreams.

◆ EMPOWER POINT – I HAVE A DREAM

What dreams do you have? How long have you had them? How does it make you feel when you think about them? I want you to write down your dream as if it has already happened. Imagine what it feels like to achieve it. Paint a picture of that wonderful moment.

My dreams are…

I have dreamt these dreams for…

It feels wonderful to achieve my dreams, let me tell you about it!

GOALS

Having goals is an important part of building focus and an essential part of achieving your dreams. For instance, one of my dreams was to write a book about life because up until that point in 2008, I never had a voice. I never attempted anything like that before so I planned what I wanted to write about and set mini goals to get it done. It was a tough process; it took two and a half years for me to complete my book and I am sure it may have been done slightly quicker if I had set specific timescales to get it done. What started as a goal of just expressing my voice as a way of empowering myself has ended up empowering women and men all over the world. My autobiography, 'Daughter Arise' is now 8 years old and still continues to touch lives and reach new audiences. It is one of my best personal achievements and it helped me to finally realise that I am not defined by my past.

What I found in the past was that when I didn't have something positive to focus on, it left time to ponder on the negative things that happened in my life. I have a list of life goals that I wrote down twenty years ago. On my list it had things like lose weight, write book, buy entertainment system, go to America, etc. It was a mix of different things and do you know, I have achieved every one of them except for going to America and that is about to happen very soon! Having goals is good. It does not matter how long it takes you to achieve what is on your list, it is about you having something positive to work towards.

In order to pursue your dreams, you will need an action plan of mini goals; a step by step plan. Maybe you only have one goal but it is yours – own it. Once you reach your goal, you will discover, as I did, the satisfying feeling of accomplishment. The feeling of doing something you never thought you could do is powerful motivation to discover new aspirations, goals and dreams.

◆ EMPOWER POINT – GOAL LIST

Write down a list of the goals that you would like to achieve in your life. It doesn't matter if it is one thing or several, and there is no time limit on when to achieve it. Write down a plan of action (what it will take to achieve it – research it!). How does it feel to be able to set goals? You could even make a vision board with coloured card, and cut and stick pictures and words out of magazines/ newspapers that symbolise your dreams/goals. Then you could stick it up somewhere you can see it!

MY GOAL LIST

MY ACTION PLAN TO ACHIEVE MY GOALS

CELEBRATING SELF

I am a hard worker and quite driven and I like to get things done and completed to a high standard. I have achieved much success in many areas of my life and everything I have accomplished is a huge achievement for me. Everything I have done has required great personal sacrifice, effort and focus. You would assume that I would take time out to celebrate and reflect on the enormity of my achievements but I have a habit of moving on to the next thing! Only recently have I started to take a pause and celebrate each goal I successfully accomplish by doing some of my favourite things, such as going for a manicure, taking myself out to lunch or even just going to my favourite place on Kings Road, Chelsea for coffee and cake!

No matter how big or small, celebrating your success is an amazing confidence boost and will spur you on to accomplish other goals that you have. Celebrating self is also about spending time doing activities and interests that enrich your life; it does not have to be expensive. I encourage you to celebrate your achievements; you are worth celebrating.

◆ EMPOWER POINT- CELEBRATE!

Write down five celebratory things you can do to mark achieving your specific goals and dreams. Next time you accomplish something, choose something from your list. It does not have to be expensive – it is all about celebrating you!

MY CELEBRATORY LIST

Things I can do when I achieve my goals and dreams:

(DIARY ENTRY – JANUARY 2001)

To love me means loving all of myself, but the inner child makes me feel insecure about me most of the time; I cannot accept her.

ACCEPTANCE AND AFFIRMATION

I struggled with accepting myself for a very long time. For many years I became obsessed with trying to fix me because sexual abuse left me feeling dirty, ashamed and inadequate. I felt there must have been something wrong with me to have warranted my dad's behaviour and I believed if I could fix the problem, then the abuse would stop. It never stopped and from that point on, I struggled to believe I was worth loving and acceptable. I constantly thought negative thoughts about myself that I spoke into my life without realising their impact. For instance, I would say I was stupid, ugly, unworthy of anything positive (love, good relationship, nice job, etc.). I believed these statements as true because of how I viewed myself.

I started to address my negative thoughts and view of self by accessing help from various resources such as specialist counselling (psychotherapy, Cognitive Behavioural Therapy). This gave me insight into recognising the root cause of my struggle –poor self-esteem. I read books on emotional healing by author Joyce Meyer (she has several books on the subject), books on the impact of sexual abuse, and the bible where I learned about the power of words and its importance to my identity. *(The power of life and death is found in the power of the tongue – Proverbs 18:21)*. I learned to declare and speak positive words about me in spite of how I felt each day rather than focusing on how I felt in that moment. Speaking words such as 'I am beautiful', 'I am valuable', 'I have a lot to offer', 'I am a great writer', 'I will overcome my difficulties', greatly uplifted my spirit and helped me to stand in the truth of who I am.

Because I am aware of this area of weakness in my thinking, I have made a determined decision not to let my insecurities get the better of me. I know if I am not patient with myself, this can lead to me not valuing my progress or appreciating how far I have come. It takes inner strength to fight the negative voices of accusation and condemnation, but even with the insecurities and brokenness that I still feel at times, I know I am just as important as anyone else in

196

society. Whether rich or poor, famous or anonymous, regardless of my upbringing, God loves and accepts me as I am.

I remember standing in front of the mirror on many occasions, tears streaming down my face, telling myself I was lovable and valuable whilst feeling total despair and exasperation at myself. It has taken a long time for my thoughts and feelings to align with what God says about me – and I am still not totally there yet. Whilst I am still learning to love Yvonne, I do like me even though there are times I still have the tendency to scrutinise traits about myself that I wish could be better. To know I am not a mistake has helped me to accept myself and provided me with the truth about my identity and value. God loves me because he created me and, on that basis, I choose to take his word as truth and bond:

I praise you because I am fearfully and wonderfully made; your works are wonderful, I know that full well – Psalm 139:14

The Lord is close to the broken-hearted and saves those who are crushed in spirit – Psalm 34:18

Therefore, if anyone is in Christ, the new creation has come:

The old has gone, the new is here! – 2 Corinthians 5:1

Let us then with confidence draw near to the throne of grace, that we may receive mercy and find grace to help in time of need – Hebrews 4:16

But to all who receive him, who believe in his name, he gave the right to become children of God – John 1:12

For I know the plans I have towards you, declares the Lord, plans for welfare and not for evil, to give you a future and a hope – Jeremiah 29:11

My frame was not hidden from you when I was made in the secret place, when I was woven together in the depths of the earth – Psalm 139:13

The Lord is on my side, I will not fear. What can man do to me? – Psalm 118:6

So now there is no condemnation for those who belong to Christ Jesus – Romans 8:1

◆ EMPOWER POINT – SPEAK LIFE: 21 DAY CHALLENGE

Do you recognise sayings you tell yourself that are negative? Below, write the things that you say or think about yourself and how you affirm those thoughts/feelings by your actions.

Negative things I say about myself:

How I affirm those negative thoughts and feelings:

Apparently, scientists reckon it takes 21 days to form a new habit, so my challenge to you is this: for the next 21 days speak positive words to and about yourself and life. Write down alternative things you could choose to tell yourself instead when negative self-talk arises. Remember, these positive affirmations must be said in spite of how you feel day to day and must come from a source of truth; something outside the influence of your thoughts, feelings and emotions. I get mine from the bible but you may choose otherwise. You can get coloured paper or card to write your affirmations on. Stick them on your mirror or in your favourite diary or book – somewhere you will see them every day. The reason for this exercise is to try something positive and new. Here are some examples that I have put together:

'I am learning to love myself each day for I know I am worth loving.'

'Today I choose not to focus on my past; instead I will imagine and embrace a better future for me.'

'I am of real value and worth because the living God created me.'

By speaking affirmations into your life, after a while you will eventually see a change. Positive thoughts lead to positive actions! On the following pages create your own affirmations that you can use to encourage you through difficult times. If you are not sure how to start, you can look on the internet for ideas or just practice!

MY AFFIRMATIONS

DECLARATIONS

It is not enough to just think about the life you want – you need to declare what you want in your life. Declarations are about putting the stamp of your future in the here and now as truth. I use the bible at times and I make my own declarations over my life:

I am God's servant and he takes pleasure in my prosperity – Psalm 35:27

God has not given me a spirit of fear. He gives me power, love, and self-discipline – 2 Timothy 1:7

I am blessed when I come in and blessed when I go out – Deuteronomy 28:6

You could create your own personal declarations as well:

'I declare I will live a life of abundance.'

'I will have an inspiring and productive day; I will accomplish all that I set out to do.'

'I am powerful beyond measure – I have the power to choose all that is positive for my life.'

◆ EMPOWER POINT – I DECLARE

Use this space to create declarations that you are going to say about you and your life.

THE POWER OF THANKFULNESS

For a long time, I was angry and unappreciative about my life. I did not care about the fact that I survived my abuse and was still here; rather, I was upset about the way I was still here. Let's face facts: there is nothing I can do to alter or change my past, its effects or consequences, but over time I have learned a key thing that has helped me develop a different attitude in the way I think about my circumstances and life – and that is to be thankful. Having an attitude of thankfulness has released me to grow into an emotionally, mentally and spiritually mature woman. I know some people might not appreciate this sentiment and may even feel offended that I would suggest it in the face of so much adversity, but learning to be thankful no matter what comes my way has helped me find healing. There is power in choosing to be thankful about the smallest of things. It has been an antidote to complaining, as at times I have been guilty of doing this a lot – especially in areas of my life that I find challenging. My experience of life this far has taught me things can happen unexpectedly and problems, which there always seems to be plenty of, can and will happen; I have become more resilient. I now choose to be thankful about overcoming hard situations, and learning from the lessons they brought.

I have taken for granted at times the fact that I can continuously speak out about my past abuse and that my life is not defined by it. Many survivors have not been able to face what has happened to them; maybe that's your story. I have met and known incest survivors that have been made pregnant by their fathers and I am thankful I never ended up with a baby conceived in abuse. I am thankful because even though I emotionally struggle with life at times, I have never had to go back into a mental health hospital because of another breakdown. I am thankful that my children never had to go through what I went through or been in the care system; even though others tried to make it their hand, God never allowed it. More than anything, I am thankful for the chance and opportunity God has given me to reach my full potential and for the love of a real family.

I have learned to recognise blessings in times of adversity. I have not always been able to do this, but focusing on the 'could have, should have been' was robbing me of my potential to grow and appreciate the here and now. It was unfortunate that I went through the things I experienced, but they have helped shape me into the woman I am today. As survivors, we cannot change the injustice of our violation but we can change how we allow it to define our view of life.

◆ EMPOWER POINT

Try and find one thing each day to be thankful about. You will be surprised at how it will change your outlook on life. Each year, I create a 'Thank you' jar as a visual point for all that I am thankful for.

To do this you will need:
  A used pasta sauce or jam jar (washed and dried)
  A sticky label
  Sellotape or glue stick
  A felt pen
  Strips of plain paper

You can choose what you put on your label. On my label I used a coloured felt pen and wrote, 'Thank you God for' and stuck it on the jar. At the end of each day, I cut a strip of blank paper and write down what it is that I am thankful for in that day.

SUMMARY

As I finish this book I want to remind you that you are:

Unique!

Valuable!

Lovable!

Powerful!

Repeat after me...

I am unique because...

I am valuable because...

I am lovable because...

I am powerful because...

No matter where you are in your life now, this is the truth. I know how hard it is to go through each step of the journey to recovery from sexual abuse. There will be days when you feel unsure how or if you will make it. But you will make it and not only will you survive, you will thrive!

I hope that you can take away something empowering and encouraging from this book. From one heart to another, my prayer for you is that all that has held you back from your experience of abuse will be the catalyst for a new beginning for you. Never let your past define you. Never let people count you down and out; look at me! I am proof it is possible to overcome, and God willing, you will overcome your past and embrace a wonderful future. Choose life.